MW01282185

*"EVERY CHILD, NO MATTER HOW MANY, IS SPECIAL."*

# "Every child, no matter how many, is special."

ᘏ

by Stephen F. Gambescia

ᘏ

March 2016
PHILADELPHIA, PA

Philadelphia studio photographer Albert Zecca took individual photos of each child in our family in 1954 (9 children) and in 1964 (15 children). When he heard that our mother was pregnant with number 16, he said with a sigh, "Mary, it was a miracle that I got your kids to sit for the first two shootings; I just don't have the energy to do another."

*This book is dedicated to the parents,
who raised many, many children,
for their love, wisdom, discipline, forbearance,
creativity, self-sacrifice, good humor,
and good graces.*

# CONTENTS

ℭℜ

# CONTENTS
𝛚

# FOREWORD
ෂ

OUR MOTHER, THE MATRIARCH of sixteen children, was
often told, "You could write a book." With a family of that size,
she never had the time. We—the children—decided to collaborate
on a book to give testament to the gifted parents who raised these
remarkably large families.

Our parents contributed to the baby boom almost every year from
1945 to 1964 producing sixteen healthy children in nineteen years—a
miracle in itself. Who knows how many children there would be if
World War II hadn't erupted in which our father served for almost two
years with the U.S. Army Medical Corps in Germany?

Rearing sixteen children, understandably, can be challenging. Our
parents never raised their voices to each other, although they did
raise their voices occasionally at us—deservedly so. They never said a
disparaging word about an individual or a group of people—a testament
to their extraordinary faith in humanity.

This book, through the eyes of our family, shows how these big
families functioned from the multiplicity of everyday events to the
signature life events of a family. Those who grew up in big families will
recognize many scenarios in this book; those who did not will be treated
in humorous detail to large-size family dynamics, which any size family
will enjoy. For as our mother said, "A family is a family whether there is
one child or sixteen children. Every child is special."

By telling our story, we are doing something the creators of
Hollywood productions and television shows could never accurately
conceive—capturing the profound blessings of a large family. From
schooling, vacationing, playing, celebrating holidays, and maintaining
order, managing a larger-than-average family is a testimony to our
parents' amazing dedication, wisdom and self-sacrifice. And we know
they'd be honored to share this legacy on behalf of fellow parents.

## CHAPTER 1

# Birthdays are "Celebrations."

ভ

**WE CALLED THEM "BIRTHDAY CELEBRATIONS."**

WE DID NOT HAVE BIRTHDAY PARTIES in our house; we had "birthday celebrations." The celebration guests were simply the members of our immediate family. With this many siblings, who needed to invite outsiders? The immediate family sufficed to make the event a true celebration.

It was not until the second grade that one brother realized that there was a difference between birthday parties and our birthday celebrations, when he was invited to a classmate's birthday party. There were about twenty children at the party, but he didn't notice any of his classmate's siblings, which he thought was odd. He told our family how much fun he had, and how it was very different from our "birthday celebrations." They played games such as Pin the Tail on the Donkey and darts. There were countless bowls of pretzels, potato chips, nuts and candy on all the tables with a huge sheet cake and limitless servings of ice cream. The highlight was taking a whack at a piñata, and then scurrying to the floor to scoop up the candy emanating from the wounded, decorative donkey. At the end of the party, the children were given party favor bags then picked up by their parents.

When our mother went to pick him up, our brother recounted all the fun things that he did at the party, then asked our mother if he could have a birthday party. She smiled and said, "Sure, we will celebrate your birthday as we do every year. Don't you have fun at your birthday celebrations with your brothers and sisters?"

Our birthday celebrations may have seemed low-key and routine, certainly by today's standards in which kids have extravagant parties. Yet, there was at least a little anticipation when someone checked the calendar and announced that one of our birthdays was approaching. Our mother would simply ask, "What would you like for dinner on your birthday?" That was great in itself. We got to pick our favorite dinner, a dinner that everyone had to eat, for there were no special orders in our household.

After the special birthday dinner, the table was cleared and the kitchen cleaned up. Some time would pass during which we would watch television or do homework. Everyone would then be summoned back to the table. The lights would go out, and then our mother would appear from the dark dining room with candles in a cake singing the obligatory "Happy Birthday" song. It was a modest cake, but it must have been enough to feed all. After the birthday song, the birthday boy or girl blew out the candles while one of the older kids served ice cream. Now we knew for sure that it was a birthday celebration, since ice cream in our home was a rare treat.

After cake and ice cream, the birthday person was given a few gifts. Again, nothing extravagant but all the attention was focused on the birthday child. Invariably, one of the little kids would wrap up a box of paper clips or a small toy in newspaper as a gift. Sometimes, the birthday child received a gift from one of the older siblings. There was no scorecard on gift giving in our home, which continues to this day. With so many brothers and sisters, no one was expected to come up with a gift for everyone's birthday. It was fun getting an "extra" gift on your birthday or giving a gift to one of our siblings who did not expect it.

One sister developed her own gift-giving system, which literally guaranteed an off-the-shelf gift. Each birthday, she took a small statue of the Blessed Mother down from the kitchen bookshelf and wrapped it for the birthday person regardless of his or her age. She always used the same wrapping paper. After a few years, it really got old but as not to hurt her feelings, one of the older siblings would refocus the gift giving by claiming responsibility for the statue then give a gift that may be of more interest to the birthday child.

While our birthday celebrations may seem routine and very low-key with only immediate family as birthday guests, a small cake, ice cream and a few presents, we always felt like a king or queen on our special day. None of us ever admitted that we did not want the big bash birthday party that we experienced with our friends. What kid would not want the expanded version of a birthday party at a fast food restaurant, roller-skating rink, bowling alley or pool? However, some of us did ask for "a real party."

After experiencing "a real birthday party," one sibling was determined to host a traditional birthday party with friends. A few days before the event, he verbally invited several of his classmates to attend. Having never hosted an outsider's party, he did not realize that a formal, written invitation was required. When the after-dinner family celebration ended, he waited at the door to greet his guests. Nobody came probably because his friends' parents must have been wise enough to know that there was no party without a formal invitation.

About an hour after the family celebration, the doorbell rang. There stood one of his friends holding a birthday gift. Hearing the commotion, our mother asked who had arrived at which time our brother announced that he had invited a few friends over for a birthday party. Confused, our mother asked him if we did not just have his birthday celebration to which he confirmed that we had. Realizing his *faux pas*, she said that the friend could play with our brother while she called the friend's mother to let her know that we would drop him off after the unauthorized party ended.

Our brother was elated at the bag of toy soldiers his guest brought. The two boys played quietly in the basement having no cake or ice cream. The friend never asked why there was nobody else at the birthday party and left without receiving a party favor bag. We don't know what he told his parents about the birthday party, but it was truly a learning experience for our brother, since he did not give up on the expanded birthday party idea. Thereafter, he continued to bug our parents about having a "real" birthday party, just like his friends hosted.

Years later, one of our sisters planned a surprise birthday party for this brother, inviting all of his friends, including girls. Having quietly assembled the guests in the basement, all that was left was getting him downstairs away from the television in the living room. He was exhausted after having spent the entire day playing football and other sports with friends, who were actually part of the ploy to keep him out of the house and occupied while the others prepared the basement for the party.

Tired and ready for bed, the unsuspecting sibling showered before dinner then changed into his leopard pajamas. Puzzled that he had put on his pajamas so early in the evening, they advised him to dress more appropriately. Not suspecting the evening's surprise, no one was able to convince him to change his attire.

To get him to the party, our mother asked him to help her take laundry baskets downstairs. When they reached the basement, a room full of classmates yelled, "Surprise." While the party surprised our brother, his classmates were astonished to see an adolescent wearing leopard-style pajamas. Our mother smiled at him and said, "Be careful for what you ask for in life; you just may get it."

The party was a complete success. With an army of siblings to pull it off, how could it not be? When leaving the party, one child said to our mother that she must be exhausted from having to plan sixteen birthday parties each year.

While cleaning up the next morning, our sister told the birthday boy all the work that needed to be done to put together an expanded birthday party. And even though she enjoyed the preparations, she confessed that she now understood why, with so many children, our "birthday celebration" is more reasonable than an expanded party.

### "DO YOU REMEMBER THE NAMES OF ALL YOUR CHILDREN?"

When people discover that you are part of a large family, it understandably stimulates a series of cheeky questions related to temporal matters: "How can your parents afford it?" "Did you all live in the same house at the same time?" "Did you eat together?" "How big is your house?" "How many bedrooms do you have?" "How did your mother shop and cook for all of those people?"

It also brings out some off-color comments: "You must be Catholic." "You must be Italian." "You must not have had a television in the house." While not insulted by these questions, our parents maintained a sense of dignity about family matters, so they either ignored off-color comments or turned the question back, giving the inquisitor pause to consider his or her thoughtlessness.

For example, after learning about the numerous children that our mother bore, someone would ask her if she could remember all of their names. She would flip the question back and ask, "Do you remember the names of all of your children?" Of course, parents remember the names of their children.

As children, we recall watching a television program about a large family who was asked to name their family members. Oddly, the children fumbled through and could not confidently name all of their siblings. Yet the mother could. In our house, we had contests to see who could name them the fastest, without missing a name and in the correct order without stuttering. Getting the order of the twins correct was a must. *(See afterword for full list of names.)*

Remembering the names of their children, regardless of the number, comes naturally but should there be leeway for remembering their birthdays every year? On one occasion, one sister's birthday almost went unnoticed. It was early evening and about eight children were at the kitchen counter doing homework. The eldest daughter was looking at the calendar on the refrigerator. She announced to everyone's surprise, "We missed Angela's birthday; it was yesterday." Our mother was masterful in managing family affairs in a pinch, and asked her daughter, who had just turned six years, if she wanted her birthday celebration that evening with a quick-kit cake or have it the following day, which allowed for more provisions. Our sister asked if she could receive presents immediately to which our mother said, "Sorry, but no." Our sister responded that she could wait until tomorrow in order to allow time for presents. In the end, she had a wonderful belated birthday, and her "best gift" was a homemade hopscotch set from her siblings, who used cardboard backings from our father's commercially laundered shirts.

## THE EXTENDED FAMILY

Our parents were married on May 6, 1944, in a Roman Catholic church in a remote borough about fifteen miles west of Philadelphia. The wedding reception was small and held at our mother's parent's home in the same town. Our mother was the oldest of six children.

It was unusual to be dating, let alone marrying, someone from the big city. Our mother was considered a country girl, but our father was born and raised in South Philadelphia. This was a country girl marrying a city boy.

Our father was the third child and second son of five children born from immigrant parents. He attended South Philadelphia High School (class of 1935) and received an undergraduate degree from the Philadelphia College of Pharmacy and Science (1939). He attended Villanova University for two years to prepare for medical school. He received his medical degree from Hahnemann Medical College in 1944.

Our parents met at Hahnemann Hospital in Philadelphia where our mother was working as a nurse and our father was finishing medical school. Our mother explained the courtship as an unrealistic dream of our father's. When our father proposed, she noted that he had just finished medical school, the war was winding down, and he had no money. Luckily, he changed her mind.

After being married, they lived for a short time with our paternal grandparents and his two younger sisters in a row house in the city, while our father finished his internship and first-year residency in pathology. Their first child, Joseph, was born into this extended family home.

Father would say that he prayed hard not to be sent overseas, but he was commissioned into the U.S. Army Medical Corps in April 1946 for almost two years of active duty eventually gaining the rank of captain. He recalled how he felt fortunate not to have been in active combat, since he worked as a chief of laboratories at the Army Hepatitis Research Center, 120th Station Hospital in Bayreuth, Germany.

While our father was in the service, our mother decided to move in with her parents and four younger siblings. Their second child, Mary Beth, was born in this home. Our father did not see his first daughter until she was nearly two years old.

Upon his discharge from the service, our father moved our family back in with his family (who had relocated from South Philadelphia to the Philadelphia suburbs), where they lived until the birth of their twins, the sixth and seventh children. Today, it seems hard to imagine living at home with one's parents, siblings, spouse and five children.

This extended family tradition had its challenges, but everyone in our family, who experienced these arrangements, agrees that it also has its rewards. Our mother was most grateful for the extended family, as evidenced by the fact that she graciously repaid our paternal grandmother by eventually having her move in with us after our grandfather died. She lived with us for fourteen years until her death.

This tradition continued with the next generation, as it was common to have newlyweds live at home for a few years and even have children before establishing their own home. Prior to being married, one brother's fiancé informed him that they would be living at our parent's home after they married. She explained that our father and she had the discussion;

the offer was made and she accepted.

Living with an extended family of grandparents, parents, aunts, uncles, nieces and nephews is an enriching life experience. Our extended family arrangements were well thought out, reasonable, and very accommodating living arrangements for both families.

The circle of life continued, when our mother was taken care of by our brother and his family during her last few years. They sold their home and moved back into the family house.

Taking care of parents in their elder years is both a privilege and an honor. You get to share special moments with your parent or parents unlike any others, and your children experience a unique relationship with their grandparents, aunts and uncles. Nieces and nephews were not only in the family as children, but several returned to the family home for short periods of time after having relocated for college or work.

## DOES BIRTH ORDER HAVE ITS PRIVILEGES?

As with most families, birth order allows for some privileges to both the eldest and youngest siblings, and provides an objective reference point for making some decisions and creating a semblance of order. Certainly our parents ascribed to the honored and long-time rule of respecting one's elders. But if age is presented as the only criterion for making a decision or awarding justice, there needs to be a good reason.

In our house, there was little, if any, differentiation between what the girls could do versus what the boys could do. Our parents were paragons of egalitarianism. Discrimination and preferences were based on behavior not gender or age.

If anything, the women had the more privileged spot, as our father had a high degree of respect and reverence for our mother. This was also evident in his spiritual nature for he had a great devotion to the Blessed Mother. In fact, during the weekdays in the month of May, the family assembled at the kitchen table to recite a decade of the rosary. He changed his middle name from "Mario" to "Marion" in devotion to the Holy

Mother Mary and in thanks for success in completing medical school.

However, there were a few fun exceptions. There was a tradition that the eldest male and eldest female, who were present at dinner, got to sit at opposite ends of the table. Most nights, our mother held the head spot for the females at the table. During the week, our father was usually still at the hospital or conducting office hours during the dinner hours, so the male seat saw more variability, which was a big deal in our house. We all looked forward to the day when we could occupy the head-of-the-table seat even if only for a night. Given the privilege, no older sibling ever relinquished this honor to a junior sibling. If an overly ambitious sibling went to the seat too early, and the older male or female eventually showed, the penultimate eldest relinquished the seat without incident.

Another birth order privilege was the youngest and most capable child got to place the baby Jesus in the Nativity scene, which was set up in the fireplace when we all came downstairs for Christmas morning prayers.

Naturally, the oldest male and female children had a tremendous amount of responsibility. They were both experiencing their own childhood and the raising of sibling cohorts. Our mother said that they raised three sets of children: the first five, the next six, and the final five. The twins began the second cohort. Daughter number ten was somewhat on the cusp of cohort two and three; she could either live the advanced life of the second cohort or dummy down to the younger siblings.

Our brother who held the twelfth position always thought it sounded neat to make the family an even dozen, but not sure it ever got him anywhere. Our fifteenth sibling, a brother named John, did get some princely accolades at times when our mother took on a sentimental posture that he would be affectionately referred to as "John the 15th." The youngest child, Ann Marie, holding the final and 16th position, merits a book in itself. Our father's term of endearment for her was Tiger Lily because when she slept she was as soft and quiet as a lily, but when awake, she was as bold as a tiger.

At our parents' viewings, we instinctively lined up in birth order;

people appreciated the fact that we gave both name and birth order, just to help their memories along by giving a more defined reference point.

Showing deference to the older siblings came naturally. Rarely did anyone complain about taking care of a younger sibling. The youngest group at some level was well taken care of by the "oldest group." On many occasions, the older siblings woke up the younger siblings and helped them with getting ready for the day.

It was a nice change of pace to have one of the older siblings be the taskmaster when our parents were away. Each had a special talent or "way with us" that made the time that our parents were away range from very comforting to unorthodox. The eldest sister was very creative, so when she was in charge, we were challenged with making seasonal arts and crafts or a gift for our mother when she returned. This did create some concern about where we would meet for meals, since the arts and crafts quickly consumed the main dinner table, and anything that our sister had us make was a very involved project.

Another "babysitting" strategy for our eldest sister was to write plays that her younger siblings could enact. Given the healthy number of siblings, there were enough actors and actresses to pull off major productions and still have some extras. They were original plays, for sure, but usually about temporal matters—father, mother and children—and of course if you drew the short straw, you had to act as the family dog.

The second eldest sister was always joyful and a lot of fun. She had an early indoctrination into babysitting. She claims that when her friends were going off to kindergarten, she was told to stay home because our mother "needed help with taking care of the twins." Most of the younger children can't judge how she did with those siblings but with the last cohort, there was a downside because she was very strict with the meals and monitored the amount of time spent watching television. She must have started the healthy eating movement, because we learned a lot about roughage, fiber, cholesterol, and the dangers of sugar highs. All snacks needed to be healthy treats. It was a totally different routine, but worth it because she let us act silly and made us laugh.

When one of our older brothers watched us, the activities ranged from reckless play to the institution of Draconian measures. As a babysitter, he was a paradox and tortured us in myriad ways starting with meals. He did not have the sense to take the milk in from the cold, so you started the morning with iced cereal. Lunch was predictable—grilled cheese and tomato soup—at least something hot. Dinner was tragic; his servings scarred us for life. He must have thought up the most unappetizing food for juveniles, preparing red pickled beets and expecting us to eat them. Celery was given out straight up. He either did not buy or thaw out the ground beef, so instead of spaghetti with meatballs, we were served spaghetti with hot dog bites. That was a stretch, even for these third-generation Italians.

One of our older brothers owned a Volkswagen Beetle and wanted to compete against the world record for cramming as many people as possible into the vehicle. What's better than to use your younger siblings?

To make matters worse, he told us that Volkswagens have airtight interiors. When the doors shut, it created a vacuum-tight sound. He explained that the oxygen was sucked out of the car, except for the driver's seat, where there was special access to incoming, fresh oxygen. We screamed for our lives when he took us on the road. However, his prank soon backfired. Our youngest sibling had an interesting way of showing displeasure by holding her breath after crying. As her close-in-age siblings, we knew this, but our brother did not. After enough collective screaming, we warned him that the little sister was turning blue, which she was. This spooked him. He quickly pulled the car over. After our sister regained composure, he announced that he would switch the fresh-air oxygen intake to "all passengers."

If we acted up or disobeyed him, he introduced us to medieval tortures. Corporal punishment was the rule. He had us hold up books with outstretched hands or stand with our faces to the corner creating an anti-fidget chamber by leaning a chair against our backs then leaned business envelopes against the legs of the chair to detect the slightest bit of motion. "Envelopes go down; you go down," he warned. To add insult to injury, he would ask one of the youngest kids, for which he had a modicum of mercy, to scream, "Mother is home!" in which case we would dart to the door only to be duped into motion, and consequently having to spend more time attached to the anti-fidget chamber.

But we endured his culinary challenges, sick jokes, and need for quiet time because outside of temporal matters, time with our brother was comparable to an extended field trip—with an edge. He was an incessant reader with a lot of interests and could go anywhere for a bargain or freebie. In spring weather, he would play motorcycle round up. He locked the doors to the house and had us scurry to the yard. He drove his motorcycle all over the property trying to "run us over."

In winter, this brother piled us into the car to go sledding. Since there were not enough sleds, he used an old college trick—he gathered enough cafeteria trays from one of the local colleges, and we sledded swiftly down the grassy knolls in the pristine college campus snow.

Summers were the best. One time he let us help him repair and paint a dilapidated sailboat that ostensibly slept two and could sail to Florida. The reality was we barely made it across the Barnegat Bay without attracting attention from the marine police. Given that he served in the U.S. Coast Guard, we escaped every time with a warning. He taught us how to read nautical maps, flags and buoys. He invented the saying "Believe," before it became fashionable. One Halloween, when one of us questioned the existence of ghosts, he took us to the University of Pennsylvania Museum of Archeology to see real mummies. Most kids get to go to a nice playground with their older brother; our brother's modus operandi was to take the younger siblings to where no kids had gone before. We may never know how he got away with his unorthodox babysitting style, but it made us appreciate the stability of our parents being home.

This family willingly practiced *in loco parentis*; it made sense. As we grew older and had children of our own, the practice continued. Most kids have come to know and appreciate a good aunt and uncle. Our children have an embarrassment of riches in that they each have close to two score of aunts and uncles.

Naturally, there were some minor differences among our family's three cohorts. The first five were known as the "Patriots." They forged the path of life events and provided a nice training ground for our parents. They often reminded the others of this fact. Any sibling born after them "got off light" growing up.

The next five (children 6-10) were the "Mainstreams." By this time our parents had complete confidence in their child-rearing abilities, and there was no leaning on the wrong side of the boat with this group. They were raised with textbook accuracy.

The final five or six were the "Favored." Both prior cohorts had serious sibling envy of this group. Everything they did was easier from their perspective. Everything this group did not do was "getting a pass" that they never had. The "Patriots" had considerable sway over the "Favored" group, not because they were older, but because they regularly told us "I changed your diaper when you were little; therefore, you should think, feel and do as I say."

As a "Favored" child, it was understood not to mess with the "Mainstreams." You just could not trust them because they believed in the adage that all heat should travel downward and pecking order was important to keep order in the family. The "Patriots" were not as annoyed with the "Favored" getting off light; by then it was cute. However, the "Patriots" had no tolerance for the "Mainstreams" not suffering at the level they did.

By the time we all became of age, the lines of demarcation among the three cohorts faded, and it was quite interesting to see how the relationships evolved. We had the tight bond as we were consanguineous, but the psychological bond was intense for we knew we all survived, and we knew we could all "tell the stories" of the double-digit family experience. This was an honor and privilege.

### MOTHER WAS "WITH CHILD" NOT PREGNANT.

Mother always kept a dignified posture (literally) and lexicon whenever discussing pregnancies and births. She abhorred the saying that so and so "had a baby" saying it sounded too primal. She would not describe herself or another woman as "pregnant." She preferred to say that "so and so is with child."

This language style was consistently used when discussing family matters. She did not "rule the roost;" she managed the family. We were not her "brood;" we were her children. Transporting children was not "herding them." In fact, she had no desire to purchase a Volkswagen "bus" to transport the family, regardless of what cohort or cohorts she and our father where moving. Transporting children with a bus was the function of institutions, not families.

When people met our mother for the first time, they often commented on "how good she looks." We guess that they expected to see this harried, unkempt woman at her wit's end. One sibling proudly displays a photo of our parents with the fifteenth child as a reminder and a humble gesture on how good this couple looked after conceiving and delivering fifteen children. How many people would look so good after parenting that many children?

Our mother also "carried" her pregnancies very well, so well that one brother, who was in high school at the time, did not understand why our mother went to the hospital one year. He explained that our mother's pregnancies and trips to the hospital seemed "routine" having witnessed several arrivals of other siblings from the hospital. As he saw it, she would go to the hospital and "come back with a baby." Since she kept modest and dignified dress, whether she was pregnant or not, she was able to "keep her shape about her," so her figure did not change remarkably that year.

Another thoughtless comment made to our parents or to us when learning about the numerous children in the family was, "I guess your parents don't believe in birth control." Our father would reply apologetically for the lack of family planning, for he suggested that good family planning would have eight boys and eight girls; whereas, we were off good family planning by having nine girls and seven boys.

During this time, a new mother could spend eight to ten days in the hospital. Our parents were blessed not only with sixteen children, but sixteen healthy children, which were all delivered without incident in two area hospitals. This is a miracle in itself. Our mother delivered her first child at age 23 and the last child at age 43. This time period was well before today's progressive birthing practices in hospitals. There were no labor, delivery or recovery rooms, and our father was not always present for the births. Given that our father was affiliated with both hospitals, he did not spend time pacing and waiting to pull out the cigars in the fathers' waiting room. His time could be well-spent seeing patients in the hospital while just steps away from the delivery room.

Our parents were reticent about their reasons for "wanting a big family." This is not uncommon for what demographers have coined the "Silent Generation." Most parents of this era would not openly discuss their private family planning strategy as is casually done today. There were many big families in our neighborhoods, and of course the parents in this time period are called the Greatest Generation.

In our neighborhood there were also families that had only a few children, but we never wondered why. Friends were friends; we thought nothing odd about "small-sized" families. We never knew what others thought about us and when someone asked our father why there were so many children, he would turn the question back to the inquisitor, "Which one do you suggest we get rid of?"

## SHOULD WE USE FAMILY NAMES?

While naming children can be fun, there must be a lot of pressure on parents who get to name only one or two children. With a bunch to name, there is some room to experiment; you get to use a few favorites, take suggestions, or have others get a chance at naming. Today, there are myriad name books available for expectant parents to peruse as helpful tools for ideas and maybe guidance. Our family names, as compared with our mother's family names, were diametrically opposed making choices even more difficult, even though there were a lot of children to name.

The first two children were easy to name: the first boy after our father and the first girl after our mother. We were told that our mother solicited assistance from the Franciscan Sisters for naming one of our sisters. Since she was born in the hospital that the Franciscan Sisters' order sponsored, a religious of that order named her.

A family committee named our youngest sister. Our grandmother, who was staying with us while our mother was in the hospital, asked each of us to write the name that should be given to our new baby sister. We then were asked to assent the name of our choice, one by one, in a private audience with our grandmother. While many siblings share the honor of helping their parents name a brother or sister, it takes on a different dynamic when it is not simply a personal preference but something that you need to caucus and lobby for.

Generally, we used our full formal names at least until we became of age. We had our share of double first names, which again we favored using in full. Most of the girls had the default middle name for Italian families, i.e., "Marie," which parents tend to invoke when things get serious. Middle names for the boys were so diverse that there is no discernible pattern or rationale.

Today, when interacting with this family, it is not so challenging getting the sixteen siblings' names correct, but matching the nieces and nephews with the correct family, which has reached close to eighty.

## WHEN IS MOTHER COMING BACK HOME?

As with many young mothers, our maternal grandmother would run the household when our mother went to the hospital to deliver the next child. Soon after we learned that mother was in the hospital, our grandfather dropped off our grandmother equipped with a few suitcases. From that moment on, we knew that there was a new sheriff in town.

Our grandmother "only" had six children, but she did not lack confidence in managing us. She understood that "children will experiment" and try to get away with their antics when their parents were not around.

When most women learned about the number of children in our family, they became bug-eyed and held their breadth. Not our grandmother. We were impressed that this intrepid woman would not only enter the home, but stay for a long period of time. Given the number of children she had to manage, it was really entertaining. Under her charge, we got to see so many risks of misbehavior end up pretty much the same way as if our parents were home.

We knew early on not to cross this woman with the white hair. Yes, she gave us presents at Christmas (there was a period when she bought for all sixteen of us), but when she was there overnight, she was all business. Thankfully, the older brothers advised us on how to behave when she was around.

On one occasion, when three of us were sent upstairs to bed, two of our brothers mumbled something about it being much too early to go to bed, and besides, our mother let us do some kind of activity before we retired. So we proceeded to play "alligator in the swamp." The youngest brother was naturally always picked first to be the alligator. The goal of the game was for the alligator to tag (biting was permitted) someone who had a body part in the swamp in which case the alligator could be transfigured back to a human.

The kids would jump from furniture piece to furniture piece, careful not to set foot on the floor, aka the swamp. Needless-to-say, this was not a quiet game. Our grandmother shouted up the stairs for us to settle down and go to sleep. One brother thinking that this would demonstrate great respect to her, blurts out in a martial tone, "Yes mame!" The sound of footsteps coming up the stairs and down the hall to our room still resonates with us even today. Given the alligator was already prostrate on the floor, he simply rolled to the side of his bed and played possum; whereas, the older brothers where caught perched on the furniture.

Grandmother instructed these two that she did not appreciate the reference to martial rule and simply needed for us to listen. The prostrate alligator was spared as she simply picked him up and placed him in his bed. Naught a sound was heard from this male cohort at bedtime again.

Many such experiments where tested during our grandmother's tenure as head of household. Those wiser actually goaded the younger ones to commit the offenses, just to confirm that this matron would not let down her guard, not for a moment. After a few of these failed experiments, we began the incantation, "When is mother coming home?"

CHAPTER 2

# Education for the Family
℘

**THE NEWSPAPER WAS A FAMILY AFFAIR.**

OUR PATERNAL GRANDMOTHER CAME to the United States at the turn of the century from the small village of Venafro, Italy, located in Pro. di Campobasso, Molise. She learned to read and write English by reading a newspaper. She never discussed formal education; she may not have had any schooling.

Our grandmother and parents encouraged us to read a metropolitan newspaper everyday as they did. We could not understand how our

grandmother, who came to this country at such a young age (temporarily at 13 then returning at 15), could learn to speak and, at some level, write English just by reading a newspaper. We figured an important strategy in becoming an educated person was to read a metropolitan newspaper everyday. If it worked for our grandmother, we wanted to develop that habit of industry. As a result, many of us became avid newspaper readers.

Over the years, our parents explained that reading a newspaper has many benefits, including:

- Develops educational and personal empowerment (Information is power).
- Brings exposure to global information.
- Helps anticipate trends and rapidly changing current events.
- Stimulates political engagement and community activism.
- Sharpens critical thinking.
- Expands vocabulary.
- Prepares one to appreciate interdisciplinary approaches to learning about our world.

Another habit of industry taught by our father was clipping news reports and commentaries along interest areas. As we advanced in age and education, this became problematic for him as he was now reading the evening newspaper with several holes in it; we took his lesson seriously. To resolve the problem, we agreed to simply mark the story of interest then cut it out the next day.

To this day, this practice has become a habit known as "clipping for success" in which we simply create files of our interest areas. As our files grew, we began to see subthemes and create more files. These files were not only interesting to read but became part of a mature, lifelong learning strategy and assisted in any further writing or research in formal schooling. Clipping files helped when following trends in areas of interest; acted as a springboard to write a letter to the editor or a commentary in a newspaper, magazine or professional journal; or identified primary sources on a subject and experts in a field. Most important, the clipping files assisted when examining various perspectives of an issue.

One down side to having the entire family practice this habit was there was only one paper delivered to our household. For years the household got only one daily paper, *The Bulletin*, which was delivered anytime after 4:30 p.m.

Whoever got the paper first was in a position of power. Our father was not home from the hospital or the office, so anyone had free rein to secure the newspaper first. Then there was the added challenge; our grandmother was an avid reader as well. If we had the paper she used the good ole' Catholic guilt trip to get it from us. She said that she had to look at "the dead ads" to see if any of her friends had passed away, since she would be mortified if she missed a funeral. This was a sobering explanation, so we relinquished the paper.

We tried clever tricks to get the paper first: Some waited close to the curb for the paperboy, weather permitting, or some hid along the side porch. Then we avoided going through the front door, as our grandmother was up to the same trick and waiting. If you really wanted to see a section and didn't get the paper first, you could barter for a section—sports, lifestyle, funnies. The funnies were a premium section, so you likely had to do someone's chore for the day to get to read them.

Our father gave up and started buying another city paper—The Philadelphia Inquirer—from the hospital gift shop. When he came home with another paper in his arm, my mother would ask, "Joseph, why are you buying another paper; we have one delivered here." Our father explained the challenge of sharing a newspaper with so many children, who became avid readers. Our mother's response was, "There were worse things they could be doing with their time [than cutting up a newspaper]."

## HOME SCHOOLING

Our grandparents were fortunate to have sent all five of their children to formal postsecondary education, including two to medical school. This is hard to believe given that our paternal grandparents were immigrants during the depression. We only knew that our grandfather was a tailor. We assumed he was a good tailor or maybe a fine tailor for the wealthy, because they seemed to weather the depression relatively well.

Naturally, not only formal education was important, but also along with religion, it was a constant in many ways and at many levels of our upbringing. Our father graduated South Philadelphia High School in 1935 and was inducted into its Hall of Fame. He received an undergraduate degree from The Philadelphia College of Pharmacy and Science (1939) and attended Villanova University for two years to prepare for medical school. He received his medical degree from Hahnemann Medical College in 1944. At age 61, he pursued his second avocation to become a deacon in the Roman Catholic Church and undertook five years of master's level studies at Saint Charles Borromeo Seminary in Philadelphia.

Certainly being concerned and attentive to a child's education is nothing remarkable. And there are enough stories in the popular press, and even in scholarly research journals, that parents may be going overboard to get their children the best education. What was remarkable in this family was that the goals, objectives, and most especially the strategies stood for each child, from the first to the last with the intensity never waning. What made our family remarkable were the educational enhancement strategies that our father would employ to get us excited about education. For him, education was a way of life.

Our father became a full professor of medicine at age 42 within Hahnemann Medical College, where he taught third- and fourth-year medical students courses in internal medicine. Medical students often came to the house for a consult. When we answered the door, there stood a medical student looking distraught, asking for Dr. G. We would escort the student to our father's study. Our father closed the large, pocket-sliding door and after about an hour, the door would crack open and the medical student appeared settled. We were never sure if he helped the student stay in medical school or assisted in the discernment that the student should leave medical school. We only knew that the student left in peace and did not return. Knowing his post in academic medicine, young scholars always asked if he could get them into medical school. His response was always, "Yes, I can get you in but let's talk about whether or not you can stay in."

## EDUCATION STARTS WITH THE RIGHT TOOLS.

Our father's strategy to get us excited about education was to equip us with the right tools; therefore, nothing was spared. The foundational tool was a desk.

Everyone of school age had to have a working desk. Studying at the kitchen table, in a lounge chair, or propped up in bed was unacceptable. And, God forbid, doing homework in front of the television never happened. His precedent for doing homework was being well positioned at a desk, feet flat on the floor, back straight and light positioned in the proper spot, ready to work for hours.

Most kids think about the coming of age as getting their first two-wheeled bicycle. But for us, it was getting our first desk. It undoubtedly made us well prepared for the close confines of college dorm life, because with several beds, chest of drawers, and desks in a room, there was little space in which to move around. Maybe that explains why we spent so much time jumping on the furniture.

Once the desk arrived, there was a lot of effort and excitement in filling it with the proper equipment to assist with our studies. A big dictionary—never a pocket dictionary—and a sundry of other reference books had to be only an arm's length away. Pencils and pens, certainly, but a classroom-style pencil sharpener was assuredly secured somewhere in the room. Protractors, compasses, slide rules, industrial-size erasers, and the full complement of school-required materials were brought in. It seemed somewhat redundant in our minds, but our father believed that it was important to have just the right station on which to conduct our homework.

The experience was a mixed blessing because we felt special knowing that we have come of age. Having new things in the room was exciting, yet the total package was a little intimidating. What is the purpose of a protractor? We were given a tour of where the books of knowledge were in the house, which always started with our father's study (the main library) and continued onto every floor and many rooms in the home, as if we had our own free library. In the later years, after our father exhausted all free space in which to place a bookshelf, he began to order portable book shelves that could be wheeled from his study to other parts of the home.

One summer, our father hired his grand nephew, who was in high school, to do work-study for him. The project was to organize and catalog all the books in our home. It took the full summer to complete. It was a little overwhelming, but when there was a "classic book" assigned for reading, there would be several copies available in our house, without fail. We could not only secure the book quickly but also offer one to a friend.

**THE STUDY**

We have to say that our father practiced what he preached. His study was well equipped and rivaled a small library. This room was sacred ground, but ground that everyone could enter and share in the wealth. His desk was symbolically a centerpiece but, as a practical matter, was too stocked with papers to sit and work. Sturdy shelving was constructed on every wall and from floor to ceiling. There were several step stools, and if you could not reach something, you recruited one of the little siblings to climb the shelves and fetch a book.

When our father took an interest in a topic, books soon followed. He had medical books, of course. We rarely touched these as the older kids felt the need to give us a preview of medical education by showing us *Diseases of the Skin.*

Both of our parents were very pious in the positive sense of the word and extended this devotion to rich theological and philosophical readings. Therefore, there were many books on the works of or about St.

Thomas Aquinas, St. Augustine, and the spirituals exercises of St. Ignatius of Loyola. There were shelves and shelves of prayer books. Naturally there were a lot of books about Philadelphia's saints: St. John Neumann and St. Mother Katherine Drexel. We thought that this prodigious collection could give us some advantage when picking a report topic for school. However, discussing a topic for a religion report with our father proved to be risky. We'd settle for something such as the virtues of the Ten Commandment; he would pull works such as St. Thomas Aquinas's *Summa Theologica*, St. Augustine's *The Confessions*, or St. Ignatius's *Spiritual Exercises*. It was safer to go to the local library instead.

The reference sections of the study were impressive and very helpful. Oddly, we had two sets of *Great Books of the Western World* by two different publishers. Maybe it was because our father was worried about having a run on us reading some original works by the likes of Herodotus, Plotinus, Rousseau, William James or any of the other great thinkers in this fifty-four volume set, or someone having to wait too long to read them.

We had encyclopedias starting at the elementary level (Art Linkletter's *Encyclopedia*), working their way up to *Encyclopedia Britannica*. This included every *Year Book* since 1957. We had a full set of the *Catholic Encyclopedia*. There were shelves and shelves of *National Geographic*. When *Time* or *Life* offered a special reference set, we would be the early adopters. We had the spectrum of reference books on space and the planets, animals of the sea, mammals, reptiles, great composers, the railroads, history of every American war, how the West was won, just to name a few. We had great reference texts on Greek and Roman Mythology.

The literary sections started in the study, but over time had to be moved to other locations of the house. So we had the litany of the great literary classics from Aeschylus's *Prometheus Bound*, to Chaucer's *The Canterbury Tales*, to Henry Melville's *Moby Dick* to most of the Shakespearean plays, to Henry David Thoreau's *Walden*. *Cliff* and *Monarch* notes were strictly forbidden and regarded as contraband; the older siblings sold them to us on a black market. Little did we know that they were actually sold at bookstores.

No school textbook was ever thrown out. Instead, they were moved to the third floor attic. So you can imagine the weightiness of series of textbooks such as Latin I, II, III, and IV; French I and II; American History, Parts I and II; algebra I and II; geometry; IPS; and some chemistry and biology texts.

Our father's study was actually a sanctuary. One could claim to go to the library at any time of day, even in the middle of dinner. The declaration of "I have to look something up" provided diplomatic immunity. Upon entering the library, one's status and station were neutralized, which was useful for an excuse not to attend an event, meet with certain people, or do a chore.

Our father reveled in the competition of someone saying a big word at the dinner table and the little kids jumping up to look it up in the dictionary (although our mother did not appreciate this, especially if she just sat down to dinner after serving the group). We would run to the study and see who could look up the meaning of a work before the others.

We had the "mother of all dictionaries"; never did you see a dictionary of this size. It was a tome. It had its own shelf and special lighting, and the bulb never went out. It would take two hands to close it; it was humongous. There was a step stool before the shelf inviting the youngest to join in the search for words. Being in the study was serious business, and it was permissible to stay as long as you liked.

By the time the last child was born, the study (library) was fully mature and our father was contemplating a master plan expansion. A breakfast nook in the house had a full wall of shelving where our mother kept some of her collected works, especially unique green bottles. Our father eyed the space with envy knowing that the location would be a perfect fit for a series of books, just a few steps away from the main kitchen table. Our youngest sister tells the story that she was in a friend's house and asked her where their library was located. She said down the street, of course. She looked perplexed and her friend made sport of her to her mother saying isn't it odd that a daughter of a doctor doesn't know how to use the library.

## CHECKING HOMEWORK.

Our father was the homework police and made checking homework more of an art than a science. He had the knack for asking about homework on the very days when we may have skimped or struggled to get it done.

Now, given the many years of his education and being a full professor in a school of medicine, one would think that he would be a sure stop for remedial help. Not necessarily. With him, all educational support sessions must start at the beginning. So, if we were struggling with a series of algebraic equations, his first question would be "What is a set?" You think to yourself; that is so elementary. All I want to do is finish these ten problems and be done with it. Not for our father. He felt the need to establish the baseline for every subject. Or he may go many steps further in the learning and tell a long story that he says we will find "fascinating." So if you were struggling in Latin, he would talk about the fall of the Roman Empire. As time goes by, hanging in the balance are the several problems or exercises that you still need to get done before school starts the next day.

There was another spot check of our academic progress. The query was fair game not only on school nights but also on weekends, holidays, and summer vacation. The question that affirmed or denied our academic integrity was, "What book are you reading?" We had mere seconds to come up with the title, and if the title was produced with any hesitation, as would go the Spanish Inquisition, we had to produce the evidence that we were faithful readers. If the response was disingenuous, we could either scamper upstairs to get "the book that you are reading" or admit the heresy in which case we were asked to select a book from the study or one of the several satellite libraries in the home and begin supervised reading sitting at the kitchen table.

The rule was to read a book a week. Outside reading, that is, not simply our assigned school readings. And during the summer it was two books a week because "you have much more time to read."

For some reason, one sister never caught on. When asked what book she was reading it was always *The Great Gatsby*. When asked to get the book, she always pulled another book from the shelf and explained how she was reading the aforementioned book but lost interest and "began another book." When asked the following week what book she was reading, she replied *The Great Gatsby*. It is uncertain if she ever got through one book, but this strategy somehow kept her from supervised reading.

## FATHER'S QUIZ SHOW

Much has been written as commentary and in academic literature about the importance of families coming together for dinner. It is considered a time to enjoy each other's company and leisurely converse about the neighborhood, school, or current events. In our house, dinnertime, after prayer, was quiz time.

Our father was copywriter, game show host, adjudicator of the correct answers, and grand cash prize awarder (which we rarely saw him do). Granted, it was not that we were not smarter than the average fifth grader; rather, it was our father's affinity to ask questions that were, in our opinion, trick questions. Brainteasers were challenging enough, but his questions had to also have some moral lesson.

One example was: "How many theologians are in hell?" Naturally, the younger children gave the right wrong answer, which is "none." The moral was just because you are a theologian does not mean that you have received grace and will have everlasting life. Another famous question was: "If you knew that you had only two weeks to live, what would you do?" We enthusiastically offered a number of exciting one-last hurrahs, e.g., go to Disneyland; travel across country; take one last trip to the Jersey Shore; or eat, drink, and be merry. After we exhausted the list, our father suggested that if we had to do something radically different than what we are presently doing, that we should reconsider our present station in life, because we should be "living the good life" now. This is certainly a tall expectation for youngsters in their formative years, but we got the message.

Our father's quiz show could take the entire dinner hour, which of course was the point. When pressed by us to "give us a question with a real answer," he would throw out something such as, "Explain how there could be three person's in one God?" or "Explain the transfiguration or the Immaculate Conception?" We kept our eye on the prize—a Kennedy half dollar, five dollars, maybe twenty dollars—but usually to no avail.

We would have to classify his moral standing as Calvinistic rather than one looking at distributive justice. It did not matter how old you were; if you did not give the correct answer, you did not "win a prize." There were a number of us who never walked away from the table with a penny. After our father passed away, several of our cousins remembered our father for the bittersweet times of asking these intractable questions.

Our father did not graduate from a school of education, but mind you there was some John Dewey envy about him. He managed to test us for every educational fad that was used at the time. We think he invented the Sustained Silent Reading program. To prepare for the summer, he would invest in major reading, vocabulary or mathematics programs. While we were packing games for the seashore, he was packing language skill building books for us. He had his own little learning center going on within our family.

One summer he distributed a box of index cards and asked us to write down every word that we did not know from reading our books, give the definition, and then write a sentence in which the word was used in the book. One sibling slacked off and pulled an all-nighter to catch up on the words, but all of his words began with either "a" or "b." Our father knew something was not right.

## FORMAL SCHOOLING—ELEMENTARY

Our formal schooling was similar to most families of that era. We had one cardinal rule: "What happens in school, stays in school, and what happens at home stays at home." It protected us from getting into double trouble when something went wrong. If a sibling started to retell an incident from school that day—"When so and so got into trouble with a teacher or the principal"—our mother would cut the tattler off and simply recite this family cardinal rule. Unless the phone rang or a note came home, our parents did not ask, and we did not tell, about how the school day went. Besides, they were running their own little school of sorts.

The start of the school year did not unsettle my mother. She figured securing a protractor or a compass, or getting books covered was doable. She was not going to be thrown off track and knew that given 180 days of this schedule she had plenty of time to readjust.

Getting school shoes was a major event but our mother took it in stride. Eight to ten kids would pile into the station wagon chatting about what would be permissible or not permissible to wear this school year (as if any of it ever changed). There was always the rumor that the bigger kids had more latitude in choosing a shoe. However, when we came home, there were saddle shoes for the girls and Buster Brown black shoes for the boys.

Three shoe salesmen helped my mother with the task: two checking sizes and fitting, while the owner ran to the back room for another pair. We sat in oversized chairs while our feet dangled. We slid off the chairs and jumped straight up countless times, yet these men never complained or told us to sit still.

My mother never double-checked any of the salesmen's decisions. She had total confidence in their ability to push down on the shoe to feel our big toes. In some ways the visit to the shoe store was relaxing for my mother. She could sit back and watch three people handle the eight to ten children without having to lend a hand.

The visit never seemed rushed; there was no pressure and each year we walked away with a new set of school shoes. When I was older, I recall going back to that shoe store and talking to the owner about the experience. I guess I expected him to say that we carried on in the store and he really had to mentally prepare himself for the onslaught of the kids. He smiled when I told him my name and simply said that my mother was a saint, for sure. Whatever the true details of our family shoe-buying excursion were, the result was the same: Our mother always held it together, especially in a public place.

Covering books for such a large group of school-age children was analogous to wrapping gifts for Christmas but more difficult because of the aggressive turnaround time. It was mandatory that books be covered by the time they were to be used in class.

The process was a production. The main dinner table was cleared. Someone went to the walk-in pantry and took out all of the paper bags collected from food shopping of which there were plenty. As a matter of fact, we probably had as many paper bags as the food store itself. Scissors and tape were premiums but with enough hunting, we found them. An announcement was made that the covering process would begin, which meant we had to gather all of our books. The older siblings naturally helped the younger ones, but not before everyone had a legitimate shot at covering their own books.

Learning how to cover a book was one of those coming-of-age talents. It looked so easy, until you tried it. The older children eventually graduated to contact paper, which left little room for error.

While covering the mounds of books, we talked about how hard or difficult a subject would be, but more interesting was the discussion about the particular teacher, usually one of the Sisters of Mercy. There was rarely a consensus on who was hard or who was easy as a teacher. Discussing the pedagogical strategies of these teachers was fine, but utter a disparaging word about any religious sister caused our mother to chime in. "That's enough of that talk. You should be grateful for what these sisters are doing for you children. It's not easy being a teacher. I admire them; I sure could not do their job." There must have been a conspiracy between our parents and the religious sisters, because whenever one of us got a private moment with a sister at school she would say, "I really admire your mother for what she is able to do with you children; I don't know how she does it."

Our teachers had a saying for the legacy students that the faces do not change, only the names. This was true for our family. While the eyes or nose or voice may seem the same, our parents were good about allowing us to be individuals. As close as we were and as important family ties were to them, they treated us as unique individuals. Regardless of the good, the bad, and the ugly that takes place in the early school years, our parents' philosophy was quite simple, "At some point it will be up to each one of you to take advantage of whatever teaching or learning was put before you."

At one time, we lived far enough from our school that we took our lunch with us. Our mother was making and packing lunches late in the evening. This could be as many as eight lunches at a time. Eventually, she then got the idea to double the amount then freeze one set to relieve her of the nightly production. A neighbor saw the production one night and was confused as she thought my mother had the wrong day for preparing food to drop off to the church for the homeless. She thanked the neighbor and said, "I knew there was something else I had to do tonight."

When we moved to our fourth and final home in early December, our family had a child in all eight grades. Not a good move-in time for a family with children, especially this many. Since school had not closed for the Christmas holiday, we lobbied to stay out of school until after the break, but that did not pass parental approval.

Our father wanted to make sure we arrived at our new school located a few blocks away. Our parents readied the nine of us (including the twins), and marched us in single file down the street to the school. The principal met us at the front of the building. She was very impressed that the school's new logo was on all of the girls' uniforms, and the boys had their shirttails tucked in. Our father delivered each child to his or her respective classrooms (thereafter the older ones were in charge and made sure we got to school on time).

Due to the school's close proximity to our home, we went home for lunch every day. It must have seemed to our mother that soon after everyone was off to school, we were returning for lunch. She always varied the lunch menu and was a master of perfectly timing when meals were ready. We don't recall special orders or food going to waste. A long grill expedited the preparation of meals, especially grilled cheese sandwiches, hamburgers, grilled hotdogs, or Philly-style cheese steaks. The six-range stove, which was specially ordered, was a permanent fixture fitted to our kitchen and moved from our previous home to our final home.

On special occasions, we were allowed to bring a friend home for lunch. Our home was always friendly to those who had disciplinary problems and were subsequently thrown out of the school lunchroom. Our mother would say, "What is one or two more kids at the lunch table?"

Traumatic school situations had an advantage in big families, since we rarely had to suffer alone. As the adage goes, "Misery loves company," and we had plenty of it. Report cards, for example, were a ritual and given our large family somebody would invariably not do well that quarter, but just whom that somebody would be was anyone's guess. And given that our parents were fond of communitarian approaches to discipline, if one needed remedial academic support we all got remedial academic support, whether we needed it or not. Report card day was discussed starting about two weeks prior to the end of the quarter, so forget about our parents not knowing that they were on their way.

The parish pastor, or his designee, personally distributed the report cards. He called the student's name, who then went up to the front of the room to get the card. The feedback was a smile if you appeared to be doing well, but a slight "hmmm" if improvement was needed.

When we got home from school that day, we submitted our report cards to our mother who took a look. If you did not do well or were marginal, she quietly put it back into the envelope with the same type of "hmmm" as the pastor. If you did well, she quietly talked about the virtues of working hard, and how it pays off. Then came the waiting period. It varied in time, but at some point our father would be home and carefully review each report card. The location varied, but the inevitable conferences would begin. Each child would stand before our father and be judged for his or her productivity in school.

Report cards were usually given out on a Friday, so one strategy would be to go to bed early and deal with the judgment on Saturday morning. One year, someone convinced us to wear extra underwear in case we would be "spanked" for a poor performance. Even though the extra underwear was not needed, our father gave a protracted speech about forbearance and perseverance.

The sentence for poor academic performance was simple and emphatic. We called it being "campused," a parochial term commonly used in our household to mean that you were under "house arrest" or forbidden to go outside. Sometimes, being campused lasted until the next report card, no matter what event or function occurred during that time.

The cruelty of the first quarter report card was that it came just before Halloween. Our father had no compunction about keeping us in for Halloween if we did not do well in school. One year four kids were campused during Halloween. The night before, we met to decide how to commandeer candy for the siblings who would be incarcerated for the greatest kids' holiday of the year. The child, who was campused for Halloween, had the privilege of choosing which sibling would be the solicitor for his/her candy. While it may have seemed like a crazy idea, the neighbors were glad to oblige most likely due to a deep feeling of sympathy for the child who could not go out because of a bad report card. They must have figured a little mercy was in order.

Being campused did have some advantages such as being allowed to have visitors. The older kids fared better because they had more interesting things to do when at home, such as shooting pool in the basement. Some siblings were campused for school or bad behavior so often that they became skilled at shooting pool and even made money off of the neighborhood kids through some primitive form of hustling. It was obvious that there was a correlation between how well you played pool and how well you did in school.

The incentive package to do well in school was unique. While most kids look forward to their first bicycle, bicycles were only awarded when we received First Honors. Needless to say, there were few bicycles around. This was an academic incentive policy that our father held to, no matter what. No first honors, no bicycle. Intermediary prizes for good report cards, such as second honors, did not exist. The stakes were high on both ends. Obviously, our parents wanted to send a clear message that education and doing well in school were important.

It wasn't easy to do well in school, so the bicycle reward system was tremendous for those who made the grades. When a bike arrived, there was major rejoicing. One reason was quite self-serving in that the proud recipient now had a shot to peddle around the property, maybe even go to the schoolyard and ride with friends. The other reason to be joyful was seeing success within the "herd." When one sibling got a bike and took the first victory lap around the driveway, there was no envy or animosity; there was pure joy and cheering for that sibling, who rode around and around the driveway. It was a scene fit for *Lord of the Flies*—the kids, at some point, could triumph.

## FUNDRAISERS

Regardless of the type of school (public, parochial or private), parents anticipated fundraisers to defray the cost of tuition and supplemental materials. Children eventually came home with some type of fundraising activity such as candy orders, wrapping paper, candles, light bulbs, magazine orders, and, in the Catholic school system, the annual Christmas stamp sales program.

Understandably, most parents occasionally opt to make the required fundraising goal by buying out the goal and getting a seller's prize. However, with so many kids coming home with stock to sell, what is a reasonable strategy? For us, as well as the other big families in the neighborhood, the course of action was to hit the streets and learn the trials and tribulations of a salesperson. There was no buying out the stock to help the kids and the school. Who could blame them? Just how many light bulbs, wrapping paper, Christmas stamps, or boxes of candy can one household tolerate?

Looking back, our parents were probably less concerned about the money as much as the "life lesson." They must have felt little pressure to do the buy-out strategy mainly because it made sense. If they favored one child in buying the stock, they would not hear the end of it. That didn't seem to bother us as much as having to settle for the token seller's prize almost every time there was a fundraiser. The Christmas stamp program was brutal because the company would change the prizes for the medium to high sellers, maybe a really cool crucifix, but not for the token prize. As a result, we had a stash of slim-line Blessed Mothers in our house, which the stamp company kept as token prize for years. One consolation was that the statue could be given away as a Christmas gift making it opportune for serving several purposes in our home.

By high school, it was obvious that our parents were not going to change their strategy, so in order to move out of the token prize category, it mandated pounding some pavement and knocking on doors. What made it even more challenging was competition from fellow neighborhood children also selling their school's fundraising wares. Additionally, we could not go to many of the houses because our classmates had the same challenge of selling their stock; usually only the parents with small families bought out the stock. Also we were hitting the streets of a neighborhood made up of large family Catholics (see first point) and Orthodox Jews, so any secular product, e.g., Christmas stamps, where not a good fit and why would someone of a different faith buy something to support Saint Elsewhere school? Our parents never pointed this out, giving testimony to their lack of any religious prejudice.

What we learned on the streets was really what any salesperson knows: When you go door knocking for sales, expect all kinds of responses. There was no correlation between which front doors were slammed and the homeowner's religious persuasion. So behind a veil of ignorance, we went knocking hoping that some stranger would be willing to give an industrious kid a break. One brother took bragging rights for years saying he would not be denied a shot at a good prize at his high school fundraiser. When the high school's sweepstakes raffle started, he worked the streets three to four hours a day. An amazing thing happened. Given enough effort, he learned he could sell raffle tickets and then some. He had no delusions of being the top seller in the high school but by the end of each week, he was turning in more and more tickets sold. His homeroom became one of the top sellers and excitement began to build. At the end of the program it was announced over the loud speaker in school that he was the top seller of the raffle tickets for the entire school. One of his classmates insisted that his parents "bought out" the tickets because his father was a "rich physician." Little did he know. Our brother ends the tale saying he was thankful to our parents for letting him lose to discover for himself what a good habit of industry could bring, even if only from the mundane raffle ticket program at high school.

Then there's other activities generated by schools and in our case multiple grade classrooms, such as card parties, parish parties, PTA meetings, back-to-school nights and field trips. Somehow our parents managed. Occasionally, our mother would attend field trips at times to lend a hand. She would not admit it, but we could tell that she was given the "challenging students" to take in her group. The teachers probably assumed there was little she had not seen, so they should take advantage of her skills and talents. After each field trip she would comment on how challenging it must be to teach in the schools and admired the teachers for what they did.

We can say that we were not asked to account for any of our parents' actual or perceived "lack of participation" at school functions. More meaningful and telling is that our parents, especially our mother, never sighed the "Woe is I" for not making a social event because she was busy with running a household, or ever begrudged those parents who did go to these functions. We know that the religious events took precedence. Our parents made sure we, and they made each one from the Christmas Tableau to the sacramental ceremonies. In fact, our father was one of the several amateur photographers, including motion film, in the parish so we had closets full of photo binders and 8mm and 16 mm film reels of First Holy Communions, Confirmations, and May Processions that could chronicle the school and parish-based religious events for the full range of the Baby Boom generation.

## FORMAL SCHOOLING—HIGH SCHOOL AND COLLEGE

Our parents were firm believers in single-sex education for high school. To those outside the Catholic school system, this may seem like a double whammy. The girls attended a private Catholic girls school run by the Sisters of Mercy. On the other hand, the boys were destined to more experimentation as they were distributed among three all-boys schools—one taught by the Jesuits, another the Augustinians, and yet another by the Christian Brothers.

This created a challenge for our parents, since they felt it necessary to know about the history and mission of the religious orders when justifying the sacrifices they made to send us to these schools. For grade school, we only had to learn two religious orders, but for high school, it got more complicated. The girls got off light as they stuck with the Mercy nuns whom they had for teachers in elementary school. It may seem as if it would be no big deal for the boys to learn about the founders, but the sophomoric mind of a male adolescent is dense, to be sure.

In fairness to us, most of the public high school founders' names are in sync with what you have to know anyway about this famous person whose name dons your high school, such as Lincoln High, George Washington

Carver High School, Bartram High School. But in our Catholic high schools, you have the name game. So at Archbishop John Carroll High School for boys, each prayer ends asking for the blessing of Jean-Baptiste de la Salle. Why? He founded the Christian Brothers who founded this high school. But John Carroll, the first bishop and archbishop in the United States, founded Georgetown University in Baltimore. But the Jesuit fathers run that university.

When attending St. Joseph's Prep (or the College), prayers are devoted to Saint Ignatius of Loyola, founder of the Jesuits instead of directly to St. Joseph. To make matters worse, there are several Loyola universities in the United States. One would assume that Loyola Baltimore and Loyola Chicago are named after different saints, but they are really the same person. This is similar to several Xavier high schools and colleges in the United States.

While the Augustinians may be one order, there are Augustinian Brothers and Fathers that must be addressed properly at their respective schools. If things weren't bad enough, these Catholic schools get really catholic [sic] and start using secular names. Villanova University (The Augustinians again) is named after its town location in Pennsylvania. St. Joseph's University in Philadelphia has its library named "Drexel Library," but there is a nonsectarian Drexel University about six miles from St. Joe's. One of our brothers, Mario, attended Wheeling College in West Virginia; they helped us by renaming the college Wheeling Jesuit. Our sister, Anne Marie, had us stretch more by attending Manor Junior College where the nuns blessed themselves several times in prayer, since the Ukrainian Sisters of Saint Basil the Great founded this college. Our father was Chief of Medicine at St. Agnes Medical Center in South Philadelphia and the Franciscan Sisters—the same sisters who founded an all-girls college called Our Lady of Angels—sponsored this hospital but they changed their name to Neumann College after St. John Neumann, who was a Redemptorist priest.

Many of us went on to work in health care and education so we continued the name games. For example, one brother's first job out of St. Joe's University was teaching at The School of the Holy Child Jesus in Rosemont, PA. Cornelia Connelly was the founder of a women's order, the Society of the Holy Child Jesus. He also worked at Neumann College (mentioned above) and Cabrini College founded by Mother Frances Cabrini (the youngest of 13 children) and sponsored by the Missionaries of the Sacred Heart of Jesus. He took an advanced degree at Temple University in Philadelphia, but don't be fooled; this was nonsectarian. Then he went to Regis University in Denver, which was safe for him, as it was another Jesuit School. He thought he was away from all of this by attending Penn State University, but when he got there he learned the head football coach was affectionately called St. Joe.

Many people wonder how our parents afforded to send all of us to college. Luckily, they did get a break, since there was never a time when more than two were in college at once.

Our father was a real paradox when it came to college. On the one hand, he had "your plan" for where you would go to college, unless you came up with a "better idea." For most of the girls, they were to go straight from an all-girls Catholic high school to an all-girls college run by the Sisters of Saint Francis of Assisi, which was the same sisters who sponsored one of the hospitals where my father was affiliated.

For some reason, the good counsel to the boys was more individualized. The first three boys had stints with military service, as well as attending college. While we had a first crack at the plan, our father stepped in if he saw that our decisions were not exactly rational.

Parents today spend considerable time and money, and expend anxiety over where their children attend college. Our father expended the type of capital that helped in this regard: wisdom. We were fortunate to have our parent's good counsel during an important time in our lives. As things played out we were very ecumenical in our postsecondary choosing, mixing military service, nursing school, allied health, business, law, and social sciences. Several of us even pursued advanced degrees. A few of us were actually brave enough to attend non-Catholic schools.

In summary, all of us have great faith that our parents are in heaven, as they had devotions to many, many saints and some of these were biggies! We know we are centuries away from Martin Luther getting us Catholics away from indulgences, but for the amount of money our parents paid in Catholic tuition, we hope St. Peter gets them past the gate. In total, our family had a combined 220 years of Catholic education—and tuition!

## SCHOOL SPORTS

What parent doesn't enjoy watching his/her children in sports? Even the nonathletic parents enjoy watching their kids play some type of sporting activity. Yet the problem with big families, attendance at every child's sporting events could absorb the entire weekend. Naturally, most parents experience a sporting conflict, but in the big families sometimes either/or becomes "Let me know how the game goes."

The term soccer mom or dad didn't exist then. What we had in our neighborhoods were families who practiced *in loco parentis*, so it was not so important that our parents showed up for a game, as long as some of the parents were there to cheer the team on. As expected, the parents with the smaller families tended to be present; some made all of the games and eventually became the surrogate parents. Our parents were not athletic, but they appreciated the fun in sports.

Our father was concerned about the high contact sports. He reasoned that the childhood and adolescent bones are not completely formed and an injury at a tender age could be lifelong. Football and ice hockey were high on the "We'd rather you not play" list. However, as with most kids of this generation, we played what was popular at the time and hoped for the best. Generally, our parents were not regular attendees at these events, and none of us were emotionally scarred from their slight attendance. But when one or both did show, it was a big deal.

Our father could be counted on to document the event by bringing his movie or photo camera. It was interesting to see a physician turn into an

NFL Films crewman. He was also the best-dressed sports journalist, as he donned his standard suit jacket and tie with a gentleman's hat.

Our family covered most of the major sports that were offered in grade school and high school: basketball, football, baseball, wrestling, softball, and volleyball. At the collegiate level, the boys advanced to crew, rugby, cross-country, and track and field. My mother was not so enamored with the contact sports; as with most mothers she was fearful of injuries.

On some occasions, our sports became an extended family event. This occurred when one brother's high school team played our mother's high school team. The entire family met at our maternal grandparents' house and walked to the stadium to see the game. My brother's team won. It was one of the few times when a scholastic sporting event became a family outing.

Our father was not able to attend many games but when one brother played football an entire season his senior year of high school, he made sure to attend. He also made the homecoming game on Thanksgiving. We sat freezing in the stands holding a hard-as-a-rock, Philly soft pretzel to take the edge off. When his team made the playoffs, our father, accompanied by one of the boys, snuck past the field marshals and watched the game from the team's sidelines. My father looked so official in his topcoat and hat that the security guards did not question him.

During collegiate-level cross-country and track and field events, our father attended a few meets equipped with his camera. During one major meet, he wanted to be sure to get a good picture of the runners starting the race, so he walked well behind the starter but dead center of the starting line. The runners looked up just before the starter pistol went off. One of the teammates asked, "Hey, who is the guy with the camera in the middle of the field? He is going to get run over." The gun went off and our father stood his ground and kept the camera rolling.

We are all familiar with the adage that everyone can have fifteen-minutes of fame. When it was one of our brother's turn during his junior year of cross-country in college for the spotlight to shine upon him, the light moved quickly to several of our sisters, showing that it would be difficult to leave behind the family. The sports page features columnist conducted a preseason interview about his running at the city college but the headline of the article read: "Leader's sisters back Hawks." The article gave him some kudos, but the human interest was about his homegrown cheering section, as several of the sisters would come to the meets each Saturday morning. It was not until years later his sister revealed that their interest was not only in seeing him run, but to get to know the other harriers a little better, so they could attend the house parties on the college campus.

As with most Philadelphians, Big Five basketball was a family affair. The lines in the sand were drawn early. Our father was proud of attending the Augustinian university as an undergraduate where he played the flute in the band. However, he had a deep regard for Jesuit education, so several of us went to Jesuit-sponsored schools. Our family sent great warriors into this Holy War: Jesuits vs. Augustinians. This was the sporting event of the year that commanded everyone's attention.

The Big Five basketball events consisting of five local colleges were great Philadelphia traditions (and still are). We chose our team in grade school and swore loyalty for life, even if we went to another college. If our team lost, the teasing was so intense that we did not go to school the next day; you deserved a day of mourning. Certainly college basketball rivalries were played out across most homes in America, but here we had the bleachers filled without making one outside call. To this day, none of us know what team our mother favored, if any. This was yet another example of the tremendous discipline she had to keep the peace in the family, over any personal preference.

If we added up the time that our parents spent at any of their children's sporting events, it would probably equate to the time spent by parents with smaller families. The message they sent was having a proper balance of activities in life. Sports were fun and important but could not command more attention than they deserved.

People always said we had enough kids to form our own baseball or football teams. We did get to experience such a franchise expansion. During the running boom of the 1970s, our oldest brother began running distance on the roads. Road racing was building momentum in the United States, and it was fun, even if you ran just for a t-shirt. This brother got the idea to start a family running team. He chose the name "Rapid Transit Runners." The name was literally in his face each workday, as this is what was inscribed, in part, on a passageway to his city job in municipal services building. Rapid Transit was the name of the city's old-time rail system.

The Rapid Transit Runners' logo was a stick figure on steroids. Our family caught the attention of many. The big attention getter was winning a relay marathon at the New Jersey shore. There were five legs to run. The next generation of nieces and nephews kept the name of the running team but thankfully contemporized the logo. We won first place in the family division. This stirred some controversy since none of us looked alike. Some skeptical members of other teams were doubtful we were really related. The test to prove our legitimacy? We named each of the sixteen siblings in correct order and in rapid succession. That cannot be faked.

Sports were just one of the many extra-curricular activities that parents were invited to attend at their children's schools. But for our parents, their favorite event was the Christmas Carol Night at the all-girls, Catholic school. Our mother said this was the main event that helped her to get into the Christmas spirit. She had no worries that the girls would perform admirably. However, her main concern was when our father would attend. She had to keep him awake so he would not snore. The choir director had a pool to bet at what song he would begin snoring.

Our parents always made the school's family mass and dinner. Again, this was a big deal at the girls' school. A formal invitation came by mail to the home. One year the teachers were a little behind schedule in distributing them, so they gave flyers to the girls to bring home. The three girls in school conspired to get out of yet another function so they conspiratorially shredded the flyer. They almost pulled this off. Turns out the principal knew that for the previous fifteen years, our parents had made the family mass. This warranted the principal to call our mother when the RSVP did not arrive. On the day of the mass and dinner, our mother told the girls to make sure they were ready. The principal said to our mother, no need to be upset at the girls for missing the flyers; we will put them in charge of organizing the invitations for next year's family mass and dinner.

## CHAPTER 3

# "If only we didn't have to eat."
CႬ

### "IF ONLY WE DID NOT HAVE TO EAT."

THIS RHETORICAL REMARK was made quite often by our mother when she thought about food shopping, transporting, storing, taking inventory, preparing, serving, and cleaning up meals. She would say this with a slight sigh, but never in a resentful tone. This, in itself, was amazing. The comment was quite practical because the food preparation in our house required considerable time, attention and care. And our mother added plenty of loving care.

How we managed meals as a large family is probably the most popular query and area of interest that people seek to learn about. Although some of the tasks were remarkable, generally ours were no different than any other family. Our mother liked (or disliked) food shopping, preparation, and cleaning up about as much as any parent and would simply say, "I guess I food shop and cook a bit more than most [other parents.]"

### MAKING THE FOOD SHOPPING LIST.

Developing the food list was more of an art than a science for our mother. It's another testimony to how she was a master at managing a large family. At times there may have been a list on the refrigerator, but there was nothing better than the list that was in her head. We don't recall many times when we were "out of something."

To compile a food-shopping list, our mother used the same strategy that she had for so many other tasks: get someone involved. Without hint or warning, she would ask someone to grab a piece of paper and pencil to make a list of what we needed to buy at the store. So, one of us simply sat at the table and made a list as mother walked from food storage area to food storage area calling out food items. The one challenge was hearing her in the deep part of the walk-in pantry; her voice faded there.

There was no personal advantage to being selected for this job, as we did not think it worthwhile to write a favorite food item. This was not one of the areas for us to express our individualism. However, the list maker did attract the attention of the siblings who would interject to list items that were clearly off script.

Our mother did not practice couponing. Sure, she cut, collected, and used coupons, but probably no more than most shoppers. She did go to several stores, explaining that this store may have better items and selections than others, or that store had the better sale items. There was the occasional stop at one store for a major food run, and then there was the episodic, "I am just going to run in for…" store stop.

**GOING FOOD SHOPPING.**

An interesting ultimatum that our mother expressed was, "I don't mind shopping, but I am not going to carry all of those grocery bags to the car, load them, and carry everything back here to our home." If we wanted to have food in the house, the deal was that someone, preferably several recruits, had to accompany her to the store, since she did not wish to undertake this venture alone.

Once at the store, our mother invoked the science to grocery shopping. Starting in the parking lot, she felt an entitlement to getting a "good parking space." She was strategic about "saving steps," and the closer to the front door of the supermarket, the better. Being a woman of great faith, she sincerely believed that the Lord would watch over her and clear a space for her station wagon. If the spot did not immediately appear, she began to pray to the patron saint of parking spaces. Who would think that there would be a patron saint of parking spaces? (Apparently, it is Saint Gemma, a late 17th century Italian girl who became a cloistered nun. The story is that she spent most of her time in prayer and did not mind occasional appeals for mundane favors, such as finding our mother a parking space.)

Upon entering the store, our mother secured a shopping cart. If it was a serious shopping day, she asked one of us to grab a second cart. In keeping with her style that families should not be run like institutions, she thought it gauche to pile groceries high and overflowing.

Once in the store, her skill of preserving every step was put into action. She knew exactly how to move efficiently and effectively around a grocery store, given her own built in GPS. She explained all of the tricks that the food marketers threw at shoppers refusing to fall prey to their gimmicks. When selecting products, there were no long discernments; she knew how to size up what was on display. We never felt the need to throw in extras and make a scene as may be played out so often when kids are "helping" a parent shop at the supermarket. When there was a new product, our mother consulted us; she was open to trying new products—within reason. When there was an oversight of an item, she sent us on a mission to get it; there was no turning back once she passed an aisle.

Safety was always first for our mother, and she was conscious of the other shoppers. There was no standing in the cart or stepping up on the lower rail to hang from the cart. According to her, "A shopping cart is simply not a toy." She was able to maneuver several children around the supermarket with ease. No child ever went missing causing us to wonder if mothers do have eyes in the back of their heads.

At the checkout line, our mother explained how she would unload the groceries on the belt for optimum packing in the bags and organization for the eventual unpacking of groceries back home. She instructed us to put the price of each item face up so the checker could see it thereby avoiding spending half the day in a checkout line.

Every bag was packed with efficiency in mind—the frozen foods, the refrigerated foods, the hard dry goods, and finally the delicate or crushable items. Bag after bag was loaded. "How about something from the candy rack at the checkout counter?" Don't even think about it.

Once out the door, she had to decide whether or not to get the station wagon to be closer for loading. We never understood the criterion for the loading decision. When the carts got to the station wagon, the back door swung wide open. Our mother's first directive was, "Somebody better climb in there and take these bags, because I am not going to throw my back out in a supermarket lot." (We never did find out where the better place would be to throw your back out.) The ride home was always without incident; no bag shifted and nothing dared to spill. Up the driveway went the car, and the next phase began.

## PUTTING THE FOOD AWAY.

Once the station wagon filled with groceries was parked, the next predictable direction was, "Go inside and get some of your brothers and sisters so we all don't sweat [or freeze; depending on the weather] to death taking in these groceries." The bags were carefully moved from the car to the kitchen table. Anyone working at this table was asked to move. This is when we were reminded just how many siblings we have as everyone converged on the bags, digging in and unloading the groceries in hopes that something interesting would pop out.

Our mother never coached a sport in her life, but she could direct a team of children on how to unpack groceries in minutes. One person was assigned folding the bags, which were then stored in the pantry to be used to line the sundry of trash cans throughout the house and for higher-level utility such as school book covers.

The temptation to hide a special item was overwhelming. If you did manage to hide something and went back to look for it, it was moved to its rightful place. Our mother had "errant goodies" radar. She spent just the right amount of time at each food storage station, always making sure that nothing went bad and everything was accounted for.

It was easy to get distracted from our chores, especially with the constant activity generally found in big family homes, and unloading groceries was no exception. For example, we knew if the phone rang, don't answer it; this was important work.

There was nothing unusual about the setup or size of the kitchen cabinets, just more of them than most kitchens had. We did have one full-size refrigerator without a freezer as well as a full-size chest freezer in the back kitchen. A second refrigerator was in the basement. We did not mind being sent down there to deposit or get an item, because there could be a surprise item being stored—maybe a can of soda or fruit cup.

Managing food storage was made easier due to a large, walk-in pantry that had shelving all the way to the ceiling and a step stool, which the adults used as well. Upon entering, it resembled a fallout shelter survival room. For us, it provided many hiding places especially during the holidays. Also, while trying to hide something, we sometimes discovered someone else's hiding place. There was a great regard for someone's stash, so we rarely disturbed it, but it was neat to know the other food hiding places in the pantry. One summer when treats were in short supply, a posse was sent into the pantry and out came an untouched dark chocolate, coconut Easter egg. On another occasion, it was the *Panettone* bread from Christmas. We were living large those days.

One day while unpacking the groceries, the front door bell rang. At the same time the youngest child awoke from a nap and was crying. Now with three things to do, our mother asked one of our sisters to go upstairs and attend to the baby until she was able to get things situated.

Our sister, who had a friend over for the day, got the idea to weigh the watermelon we had just bought, because they were impressed with its size. They carried the watermelon up the back stairs to the scale in a second-floor bathroom. After confirming that the watermelon was, in fact, heavy, they started the trek downstairs.

As with most watermelons, this one was both heavy and oddly shaped making it difficult to carry. In negotiating both holding the heavy watermelon and walking down the narrow back steps, the watermelon slipped. Down the steps it rolled with a thump, thump, thump, thump, thump, splash! Our mother let out a horrific scream from downstairs, thinking the girls had dropped our baby sister down the steps. When she discovered it was only the watermelon, she was overjoyed and laughed, to the great consternation of all who witnessed the event.

## START THE DAY WITH A GOOD BREAKFAST.

Most people agree that breakfast is the most important meal of the day. Not in our house. Our parents were night people. Our father worked nights between late-night office hours seeing patients or some function related to his profession or religious work. The younger children don't remember our mother "getting us up" for school. This was a job for the older siblings who also prepared breakfast. Even at a young age, we realized that our mother needed her rest, and we wanted her to be in it for the long haul. We knew not to wake them for menial sustenance.

Getting breakfast from the older siblings was kind of neat because we were upgraded from the obligatory cereal to some serious breakfast treats, such as bacon and eggs on toast or French toast. (This was where having a favorite older sibling paid off.) While our mother did not mind the older kids making breakfast fit for a king, she did have one important rule: "If you are going to cook like a king, you will also clean up like the servants, because I am not going to wash any pans when I get down there. That kitchen better be immaculate when I get down there, just like I left it last night."

Cereal was in the cabinets at ground level; it was kind of neat to get our own cereal box. Of course, whoever got a virgin cereal box also got the prize inside. More often than not someone older, who took on that mission soon after the shopping spree, excised the prize. Having cereal as a treat before bed was permissible and was also an opportune time to get the cereal prize before the morning crowd.

The challenge with breakfast was that it was rolling. With the family spread among four or five schools, breakfast was definitely a serve-in-shifts meal. A trick for the older siblings was that if you prepared breakfast for one of the younger kids, you got a pass on the clean up. Another benefit of so many kids preparing breakfast was invariably someone's ride would come early or another sibling was leaving with or without someone, so those leaving later got a ready-prepared meal. One brother lacked time management but was a great preparer of bacon and eggs with the eggs hot and the yoke dripping onto the bread. We loved those mornings when his ride came early. "Bacon and eggs anyone?"

Our mother only prepared breakfast when it snowed. It consisted of hot oatmeal—and plenty of it. Nothing tasted better than our mother's hot oatmeal on a cold snowy day. Everyone ate it (if there is a derivation for why this has become "comfort food," this must be why). We could even come down in our pajamas and have hot cereal prior to getting dressed for school.

The sound of the all-news radio station aired in the background as our mother quickly worked the two big hot cereal pots. Nobody wanted anything other than hot cereal when it was snowing.

Saturday morning breakfast was the best breakfast of all. As kids we learned the ritual. First one up had the responsibility to wake the other kids up for Saturday morning cartoons. This was especially important in the fall when the new season of cartoons started. If someone wasn't awoken, the code was violated. The problem was with so many kids to wake, chances were good that someone was left sleeping. And if someone had bed hopped that night, it was their responsibility to get up for the early morning cartoons. Those left sleeping in felt the need to share the code violation with anyone who would listen. Of course, we all had plausible deniability, as there were plenty of siblings to blame for not getting one of the others out of bed for cartoons.

Another soft violation was eating breakfast in the living room. The rule was no eating in the living room. For some reason younger siblings thought this rule could be violated for Saturday cartoon hours, which it frequently was. And we all know it only takes one kid to violate this rule for the rest to follow. That one pays double when discovered by our mother, because all of the other kids claim that "so and so brought food in first," insinuating that those that follow suite deserved a lesser sanction. Our father did not enforce the "no eating in the living room" rule on Saturdays with such vigor. Thus, there was tacit approval from him.

As children we believed an adult's idea of a good breakfast was simply coffee. We have fond memories of getting coffee to bring upstairs to our parents' room. Often we fought to see who could do the honor. It was a fun challenge, as the honoree had bragging rights if he or she could bring up a cup of coffee and not spill it on the back steps.

The back steps had a door on the second floor that was half glass. One of our parents would open the door and yell, "Who is in the kitchen that could bring up some coffee?" The call made a distinct echo down the steps and permeated all the rooms on the first floor. This started the stampede into the kitchen. Those who knew they would not make it in time ran upstairs to our parents' bedroom to wait and see if the coffee would be served without incident.

Two kids were required for each cup of coffee and an additional kid brought the milk while another brought two spoons and the small sugar bowl. The delivery order was important as the ones carrying the coffee went last, since they had all of the pressure. The outcome was fairly consistent. Significant drops of coffee were spilled on the back steps and each server claimed that "it was just a drop" and blamed the spillage on any one of the followers or those providing moral support along the long pathway from kitchen to master bedroom. There was little bickering about the spill because while drinking her coffee, our mother told us about her dreams of angels.

As we got older, the challenge to get our parents coffee grew old. As teenagers we became lazy and had no desire to bring coffee to our parents on the second floor. At that time, when the glass door to the back steps shook, everyone in the kitchen became silent. Our mother would call down, "Can someone bring us up a cup of coffee?" No patter of feet this time. She then followed up with, "I know someone is down there," then began calling one name at a time. Our trick was to simply yell another sibling's name foregoing the task to that sibling.

With the critical mass of children came an instant schoolyard, and our imaginations took over for what games to play on early Saturday mornings. A favorite game was playing swimming pool. We would layout several blankets, side by side, to make an imaginary swimming pool in our formal foyer. We swam the freestyle and breaststroke across the large foyer floor.

Our favorite game was using the long coffee table from the living room and making it the slip-sliding board by placing it on the steps, waxing it, and sliding down into the make-believe swimming pool. Surprisingly, when our father came down the front steps, he only patted us on the head and went into the kitchen for coffee. When our mother discovered our antics she yelled, "I can't have anything nice in the house; this is not a playground. Joseph, do you believe what your children are doing to my coffee table?" This Saturday morning playtime often came to an abrupt end.

The more subdued games, such as hide-and-seek and house, were common but there was always someone who wanted to ramp things up. One case involved our going to the basement, turning the lights out, and telling scary stories. The basement had many rooms and back rooms, and even a back basement, which was a genuine fallout shelter replete with can goods, dry goods, and jars and jars of water. It also contained the heater, which looked as if it could generate enough energy to fuel the Titanic. Occasionally when the heater kicked on, the doors flipped open revealing what can only be described as Dante's Inferno. There was a cellar drop behind double doors that was fit for a castle. Some of the younger siblings were concerned that this section of the basement may be where someone might go "missing."

"Dare ya" games were fun. One of our favorites was to dare someone to run the length of the back yard, around the big bush (about forty yards each way) in his/her pajamas and bare feet in the snow. Again, surprisingly our father, who was an internal medicine doctor, didn't flinch. He was amused by the sight and simply drank his coffee looking at us from the kitchen window. However, when our mother discovered us frolicking in the snow with bare feet, she cried, "You'll all catch yourself a death of pneumonia."

## SUNDAY MORNINGS

Sunday morning to early afternoon was a defining moment for breakfast in big family households. While we could get our own breakfast in the early morning, it was better to wait until we returned from church when our mother would prepare something good, for sure. Breakfast was still "breakfast" on Sundays in our household; we never used the term brunch, which was reserved for people who ate out after church.

The kitchen had an eclectic smell on Sundays. Our mother made breakfast while simultaneously beginning the preliminary preparations for Sunday dinner. A big pot of red sauce would begin brewing, since we always had company. It could be any number of relatives, close friends, or a student or resident from the medical school, who was far from home. And judging by the size of the pots on the stove, we could tell how many were expected.

Another smell permeating the home on Sunday mornings was that of peppers being prepared by our grandmother (they looked more like they were burned). To the young ones it was a sharp smell; to the older ones, who may have been out late the night before, it was a stomach-wrenching, pungent odor.

Sunday morning visitors were no surprise in our house. Sometimes to the surprise to our mother, our father would invite a neighbor to stop in for Sunday breakfast, or a friend, an associate, a priest or a religious sister would visit earlier than expected, adding to the already-overcrowded breakfast table. Yet with all the unexpected guests, our mother never fretted. We just made room for more.

Sunday morning also meant our newspaper reading rituals. Even though our father religiously read the newspaper during the week, Sundays he seemed buried deeper in the paper. As he always encouraged us to read the paper, he usually encountered missing sections absconded by a sibling who took it to the bathroom and never returned it. He would then send a child reconnaissance scout to hunt for the missing section and return it to him.

By early afternoon, the Sunday meal rituals were in full motion with every range working, the ovens (there were two on this unit) cleared of stray pots and pans, and our father reading the Sunday paper, which he spread across the table. Our mother shuffled stray children out of her working area warning, "If you people want to eat tonight, you have to give us some room to work."

The operative question on everyone's mind was to guess what kind of pasta was being served that evening. In our house, it could be any of three varieties: long and stringy, fat balls, or small balls. Over time, we learned there were numerous varieties, and we each had our favorite kind. Each Sunday we hoped our favorite pasta would be served. Needless to say, we were disappointed when our favorite was not chosen. Our mother's comeback was always, "Next Sunday we'll have your favorite pasta."

The hands-down favorite pasta was anything our grandmother made. The ritual began when our mother asked one of the older kids to go into the pantry and get our grandmother's huge cutting board. Next, one of the middle-age kids would say, "Let me get Grandmother's broom handle," which was actually a long and thick pasta roller that resembled the end of a broomstick. We would fly it around the table like a witch's broom, until she grabbed the back of our shirt and pulled the parochial "rolling pin" out from under us—all in one quick motion.

The pasta preparation process began with several chunks of dough positioned under kitchen towels. We were warned not to touch anything, since the dough needed to rise. Carefully, our grandmother set up several mounds of flour at which point we asked her, "Make your swimming pool." She cracked the eggs into the flour holds, and—like magic—eggs floated perfectly in the flour. To us, this was one of the first wonders of the world. Our grandmother then swooshed flour onto the board like a windshield wiper, which was done with such precision, better than any mechanical device. When she finally removed the towels from the dough piles, we could not resist asking, "Can I punch the dough?" The answer was always by her raising a finger—"No!" She pressed and patted the dough and then leaned on the roller and effortlessly the dough spread over the board. She grabbed a knife and with the first few cuts of dough, we then knew what kind of pasta was that night's selection.

After a few rounds, we waited for the opportune time to snatch a piece of the pasta to eat. She would smack any hand that reached for a piece. Since she was the maker, she was also the giver of the pasta. After denying one a piece, she slipped an errant piece to one of us standing behind her, as if none of the others could see. A line formed behind her, as we were all given one piece, which appeared as an unexpected gift. Overall, our favorite pasta was her gnocchi. We called them "sinkers," because the dough was so thick that the pasta sank in our stomachs. It is a taste we never had again after she passed away.

**LUNCHES ARE ALL IN THE PLANNING.**

Big families never eat lunch at fast food restaurants. Instead, planning for lunch started the night before. It was a difficult process, since it required our mother keeping track of who was in what school and who needed what for lunch. Some schools had lunch calculated into the tuition. Some of the older siblings in high school made their lunch. Most of the children needed lunch money. None of us could keep track but our mother could. There was never a complaint that something was missing. She was that good at keeping track.

At one point, seven of the older siblings attended elementary school located far from home. As a result, these siblings had to take their lunch to school. Imagine seven sandwiches lined up (assuming each ate just one), seven pieces of fruit, seven boxes of raisins, and a few cookies for each. The lunches were prepared the night before and then refrigerated. Out they came the next morning.

Someone gave our mother the idea to make a second set of sandwiches and put them in the freezer reducing her task to making sandwiches only three times a week. Imagine fourteen peanut butter and jelly sandwiches lined up on the kitchen counter.

By the time the younger kids were in school, we were closer to the elementary school, so we went home for lunch. More often than not we had a hot meal. Our mother was a master of timing. She had the restaurant-sized grill fired up by the time we arrived home for lunch, which did not play well if someone dilly-dallied walking home. The teachers knew that our mother was a master at timing and that no child would return late. This eliminated that excuse for waltzing in late from lunchtime.

## DINNERTIME

Dinnertime was the consummate family time in our household. There was no opting out of dinner or setting a different time. Timing for meals was mandatory especially when preparing a hot meal to be served at the perfect temperature.

Meal preparations were usually a family task, and our mother did not hesitate to assign jobs to anyone moving through the kitchen around dinnertime. And if there were too many people crowding the kitchen around dinner preparation, our mother announced, "Whoever does not have a function in here, get out of the kitchen; otherwise, you are going to get a job."

There was plenty to do: clear the tables (there were two), arrange the proper chairs at the table, set the table—properly—make a salad, or make a huge pot of iced tea. The table closest to the stove sat twelve with a seat for our paternal grandmother and a high, full-seat stool at either side of our mother for the younger children. The "big kids table" sat three or four on each side with one chair at the end. The seats served a dual purpose for storing games under the seats.

At some point, dinner was ready. There was no dinner bell—God forbid—no primal scream of "come and get it," no screaming from the first floor to the other two floors. Instead, our mother recruited one of the little kids to go upstairs and call their brothers and sisters for dinner without screaming.

The second floor was no problem, as this was the girls' floor. On the other hand, the third floor, where some of the older boys could be napping after school or sports, was dark and mysterious replete with peculiar sounds and smells. The doors to the bedrooms were always closed and who knows what lurked behind those doors.

The dinnertime roll call strategy was simple. Run in, holler, "Dinner!" then run like the wind back out. Unfortunately for the smaller kids, the execution came with some discussion, so the older boys knew their tentative voices meant time for dinner. This gave them enough time to devise a plan of their own—usually some creative act to scare them. Reporting this imminent danger to our mother evoked the same response, "Don't be silly; they are only your brothers upstairs." But we were convinced there must be more to them for which we needed to be concerned.

Regardless of the age of dinnertime recruiter, we assembled for dinner. There was no "wait until…" Anyone sent to call the others for dinner had the authority to turn the TV off. If anyone arrived late, the straightforward meal sanction was "bread and water."

Proper attire was required at the table. Shoes were mandatory, even in the summer. The males never wore a hat but always wore a shirt. The girls wore a dress or slacks that were fitting "for a lady." Our father did not say much about the military, but we always felt he stole a few strategies for how to maintain a semblance of order and respect.

Prayers were an important part of the meal; in fact we believed our father coined the adage "a family that prays together stays together." Most families do fine with a simple grace before meals. Not our father. Our prayers consisted of a litany of traditional and original prayers. On one occasion, our father was in his study drafting that night's dinner grace on a yellow legal pad. No index card or simple, lined copybook paper. This was a legal pad with prayers that took up multiple pages. Here was one recitation of our grace before meals.

*The Sign of the Cross:* In the name of the Father, and of the Son, and of the Holy Spirit. Amen.

Traditional *Grace Before Meals:* Bless us, oh Lord, and these thy gifts, which we are about to receive, from thy bounty, through Christ our Lord. Amen

Let us pray for all those who leave home for study or labor. Let us pray for… (At this point in the prayer we mentioned by name all in the family who left home for study and labor, including military service. Over time, many did leave ostensibly for study or labor, so the list became long until finally almost everyone was mentioned. That was many names that those at the end of the family had to recite, and there was often a discussion about which of the twins' names came first.)

Keep them, oh Lord, in the apple of Thy eye; hide them, oh Lord, in the shadow of Your wing.

Let us pray for the sick and the dying;

Shine Thy countenance upon them, oh Lord.

Let us pray for Dad's patients. (Over time this list included those in the family who worked in the healing arts.)

Recite the *Hail Mary*—the whole *Hail Mary.*

Let us pray for peace.

May the peace of the Lord be always with you and with your spirit.

May the souls of the faithfully departed, through the mercy of God rest in peace, Amen.

We then gave our family's version of the litany of saints that included:

Saint John Neumann—Pray for us.

Mother Katherine Drexel—Pray for us.

Saint Maria—Pray for us.

Grace began when our mother made the sign of the cross. Anyone attempting a premature grace was doomed for failure. During special liturgical times such as Advent or Lent, our father added a special reading. One book we remember was called *Good News for Modern Man*. During vacation, we had an added reading from a prayer book, because our father reasoned there was more time for prayer. Thus between and among easily recognized holidays, liturgical observances, birthdays, and any national crisis, there were always adjunct readings.

Dinner began after prayers. If some unsuspecting guest arrived, they had at least three false Sign of the Cross overtures. Truth be told, our mother used her peripheral vision to inspect the food on the stove, and probably secretly prayed that it would not get too cold.

Food was not placed in the middle of the table with the command to "dig in." Instead, our mother made a platter for each person. She did this for several reasons. First, she wanted to make sure a meal was served at the proper temperature. Thus food came right from the pot, pan, or oven directly onto the dish. A "runner" was assigned who ran the plates to the tables. Second, our mother wanted to make sure the portions were spread appropriately. Third, our mother knew each child's likes and dislikes. She also knew that our father had no tolerance for the dislikes. He had dramatic ways of making this point. "You should eat whatever your mother gives you. If your mother gives you sawdust, you eat sawdust." Our mother was quite thoughtful in not having us err in such direction.

Our family's tradition was for the eldest female to sit at one end of the table while the eldest male sat at the other end. Most days this meant our mother was at one end and our father at the other. On the night's when our father was at the hospital or having office hours seeing patients, the eldest male sat in his spot. A fuss ensued when a younger sibling attempted to assume the spot out of birth order. Our mother resolved the issue by claiming that the chair would remain vacant because our father may be home soon, even if it wasn't the case.

Dinner was not just for eating. We had meaningful discussions, stories that had a moral lesson, brain teasers, and sometimes jokes. There was no gossip, and things that happened at school stayed at school. If there was off-script discussion at the older siblings table or nobody was talking, our father would rise from the table, walk over to "the big kids' table," and request that he had better hear some meaningful conversation. It was not clear what the consequences would be, but the conversation resumed.

Quiz time was the best because money could be won. Our father laid coins on the table for simple questions and bills for the really challenging questions. Our problem was we thought there would be concrete answers to the questions. But most questions were brainteasers, Biblical stories, or moral lessons from an oracle. In the end, we focused less on the money and enjoyed the intellectual bantering.

The "initial game" was our favorite. The game involved our father giving the initials of a famous person, place or thing, and a line of "yes" or "no" questioning began. It wasn't a fair competition for the younger children, because their idea of something famous could be the name of their favorite cereal.

When things got loud, someone began the game *Oder in the Court*. This was our mother's favorite. The rules went like this:

*Oder in the court.*
*The monkey wants to speak.*
*No laughing, no talking, no showing your teeth.*
*No making funny faces.*

*No times (time outs) or checks (one bad)...*
*And it counts when you are eating.*

The game commanded everyone to be perfectly silent. The one who stayed quiet and unobtrusive the longest was the winner.

There were dinnertime rules we had to follow. No one was permitted to leave the table until our mother finished her dinner. Only then could we be summarily excused. No phone calls were taken during dinner. The only exception was when our father could be receiving a call on a medical matter. In this case, we were allowed to answer the phone. Trying to formalize a date or where to meet our buddies after dinner was no match for dying patients in a large urban hospital.

There was only one viable reason to leave the table—to go into the study and look up the meaning of a word. Sometimes there would be a contest to see who would get there first.

## CLEAN UP

Clean up was assigned to several teams: two teams cleared the dishes, and two teams washed the dishes then put them away. Teams worked on alternate days. The problem came when one team bartered its turn to another team, which usually led to no one being able to keep track. There were many methods tried, such as odd and even days, male and female saints' feast days. As is common for adolescents and young adults, the battles were more important than winning the war. This built to a crescendo. Finally, our mother would declare, "All right, I will do the dishes," in which case the rightful team's day was quickly resolved. Any animosity to the loser was erased as soon as the radio was turned on. It was a time of day when it was ok to have loud music. It made doing the work much easier. At times, we danced to the music—dance, dance and dance. Our mother loved to see us dance.

We never understood having dessert after dinner. The time that it took to clean up was significant enough to take your mind off of food for awhile. Dessert was something we had sparingly or a little sweet treat that the adults had with coffee. Having dessert was a special event.

The food itself was only half the fun. Being able to go into the full-chest freezer or going down the basement to the other refrigerator or walking into the walk-in pantry to get something special provided excitement, too. Sometimes something good just appeared. We were fortunate in that many of our father's patients sent fruit baskets or crates, large cakes, long-tray pies, or a five-pound box of chocolates, especially around the holidays, which is why our mother rarely baked or bought baked goods. There were cherry cheesecakes, ricotta cheese pies, poor man's fruitcake, Easter bread, *Panettone* bread, real biscotti, pizzelles, and trays and trays of Italian cookies. It was not really considered dessert; it was enjoying a little something sweet that you knew someone labored to make with great care to say thank you.

If there was dessert, the question of additional clean up came up. Should the dinnertime team be assigned or should a new team be recruited? Luckily, cleaning up desserts was not bad, so the work got done without incident.

At some point in the evening, our mother declared that the kitchen was closed. The lights went out and everyone scattered to their rooms to do homework, while one of the middle boys took the trash out to the garage. The culmination of kitchen activity ended when the chairs were flipped on the table, restaurant style, and the kitchen floor was vacuumed. The lights only went on one more time when our mother prepared coffee for the next morning. She said that she measured the aging of the family by the size of the pot of coffee she prepared for the morning. When the family was fully matured, she eventually prepared a party-sized coffee pot that served twelve.

Imagine meals on a holiday. No wonder we often heard our mother say, "If only we did not have to eat."

Our family appeared in a front page story of *The Philadelphia Inquirer* on January 11, 1965. Here we are going to church for Family Sunday, except for Ann Marie, the sixteenth, who was just born.

## CHAPTER 4

# Holidays at Home
℘

### "POLICE THE GROUNDS" FOR MEMORIAL DAY

WE WEREN'T INVITED TO MANY PLACES as a family, even during the holidays. It's not a complaint, just a simple observation. It made sense. What host could handle a dozen, maybe more, kids? Actually, it wasn't just the holidays.

Our mother once told us of a time when she received a phone call from a civic association official regarding our father receiving an award. The official invited the entire family to attend the awards dinner. While our mother was grateful, she felt it important to let the official know the extent of the invitation.

"You do realize that we have a large size family?" our mother noted.

"Yes, I heard it was large," said the organizer.

"We have sixteen children," our mother shared. There was silence on the phone.

"Let me get back to you after I discuss this with the Board of Directors," the person replied awkwardly.

Needless to say, all the holidays in our family were spent at home, which was never an issue since our parents loved holidays and hosting holiday parties. So from the casual Memorial Day picnics to the high holy days of the Easter season, holidays were always at our house and anyone could join us.

Memorial Day was fun, but even something as casual as a picnic took a lot of work. Our father's enthusiastic expression for preparing for Memorial Day was "police the grounds," which was another way of saying every piece of the outside property had to be spotless and in good order for our field day venues. The garage had to be cleaned and organized, and the cellar drop doors served as an extra access point to the house. Anyone observing the picnic preparations would think we were hosting the Olympics.

Our mother, being the eldest of six children, had a large extended family with her siblings rearing close to fifty children. Add another fifteen from our father's side, and there were sixty-five first cousins roaming the campus, not including any additional extended family members, as well as their friends, neighbors, and children's friends. That's a lot of hamburgers, hot dogs, potato salad, and Rice Krispy® marshmallow treats to prepare.

As an army veteran and the parent of sons who served in three of the other military branches, our father commemorated Memorial Day in a special way. Clean, fresh, mini U.S. flags lined the driveway and other areas of the property, and the clotheslines were donned with red and white triangular flags similar to those found at car dealerships. But the prize symbol of the Memorial Day hosting was hanging a large, clean flag from a third-floor window at the front of the house. *(See photo of family home at 141 Highland Ave. on page 134.)*

Draping the oversized flag from the window was a thrilling event. Several of the children lifted the screen in the window and placed a long pole with Old Glory on the end. Our father coached the display placement from the end of the long driveway. The flag had to be positioned perfectly, so when visitors entered the property, they knew our family believed in *Pro Deo et Patria* (Latin for "For God and Country." (Latin expressions were common in the household, and no one escaped having to take at least Latin I and II in school). If someone was standing in this position of the property, as our father was inspecting the flag, he would also see a shingle hanging from a tree with the house street number and the inscription, *Pax et Bonum* ("Peace and Goodness"), in big bold letters.

Rarely was our father without a tie even at a picnic. Decked in his noble attire, he managed the field events and awarded prizes given for water-filling balloon contests, running races, races with eggs on a spoon, and a host of other springtime challenges. The younger children would gather around our father and perform tricks to win a trinket or piece of bubble gum. When the prizes were all dispersed, one bag remained, which held the coveted boxes of sparklers—the one Memorial Day or July 4th firework that was Mr. Safety approved.

The main event took place in the playpen, a hedged-in area, which housed a badminton or volleyball net. This event brought new meaning to weekend warrior with family pride and bragging rights at stake. Pressure was especially on the older children, since the matches were the test of whose family had the most athletic offspring.

Given that every point mattered, every play was argued, even with the "best" officiating. One uncle had the temerity to serve as official and final arbitrator of each play. With a hand in one pocket jingling his change and a thick cigar, he took command of a field of scores of screaming kids and young adults. The youngest kids lined the perimeter of the court waiting to fetch each ball that went out of bounds and to deliver the ball back to the team he/she hoped would win. Others stood outside the hedged area but had no problem hearing what was going on, as the voices grew louder and louder as the day wore on. They played until dusk with no mercy for anyone's kin or friend of kin. What eventually broke up the games was an announcement that the grills, which had been burning all day, were now ready for toasting marshmallows.

With so many cousins and family members assembled, Memorial Day was also movie-casting day. Our father and assorted uncles were not satisfied with reels of film documenting Christenings, birthdays, First Holy Communions, May Processions, little league games, and picnics with their children. They tired of candid shots. Using 8-mm film cameras, the high-tech apparatus of the day, they brought new meaning to home movies by scripting the productions, recruiting a large cast of characters, drafting storyboards, and selecting off-the-beaten-track shot locations. They asked their wives to construct costumes and made lists of who had what equipment for capturing the best shot.

The first film was a short production about the kidnapping of Baby Oglethorpe. Inspired by the snappy 1925 song and the 1949 film, *Yes Sir, That's My Baby*, the cinematography was relatively easy as Baby Oglethorpe was simply transferred around the neighborhood, while the cameramen shot from one location to the next. The mothers were told the infant character was a doll, but officially an infant played the leading role. The mothers were mistakenly under the impression that the baby actor was upstairs napping. In reality, the director asked one of the children to take the baby out the back door to the movie shoot location.

On one occasion, a stop by a police officer at one location proved fortuitous. The officer was curious why several young men with movie cameras were taking shots of an abandoned baby. After much explaining, the director invited the policeman to join the cast. He was a hit.

To avoid further attention from the law, the next film was shot in a defunct western town "theme park" in Rio Grande, New Jersey. The film was a classic about when boy meets girl in a swinging western town. The antagonists turn out to be local Indians (played by several pre-pubescent boys). Our oldest brother took care of the local natives with his six-shooter. The death scene was quite dramatic; it took forever yet was a crowd pleaser. The town beauty faints with all the excitement but is revived by a tall glass of lemonade. Some still claim it was spiked.

Our father could not resist a medical theme. Thus was born *Flumor Tumor*. The movie was an early form of the game "Operation," in which a skilled surgeon took a sundry of items out of a patient's body, which was lying on an authentic gurney. The props team got paid extra to commandeer the gurney from our father's hospital. This was not the kind of movie to inspire young children to want to become physicians.

Over time, the men became more experienced and recruited more characters and edgier genres. Taking advantage of the families visiting the Jersey shore, all cousins (sixty plus) were divided into two bands of pirates each marked by a red or blue bandana. The costume mothers cleared the shelves of three five-and-dime stores purchasing large quantities of bandannas, plastic daggers and fake swords.

This filming caused casting problems in which the unsuspecting child actors thought they were going for a nice summer swim in the Atlantic Ocean. Instead, they spent an afternoon on the hottest day in July on a fly-infested dune—something even real pirates would have avoided. The older children wanted to form a union, as they were now feeling exploited.

Back by popular demand was another medical movie, *Strange Cases for Dr. Casey Killdare*. Again, the cinematography was manageable as each malady had an easy before and after shot. Shoot the oversized thumb, and then take the prosthetic off. Place dots on one of the children's faces, then slowly reduce the number of dots—basic trick photography and easy film splicing. The star of the movie was not the handsome Dr. Casey but a paunch, just-hit-puberty boy who played the witch doctor, who cured everyone—almost. Given this was another summer film, the older boys were not thrilled. That did not matter as their lifeless faces were only used as undertakers for those who could not be cured. However, they did need to wear black suits and ties on a hot August afternoon.

## THE BEST HAUNTED HOUSE IN THE NEIGHBORHOOD

The year was 1967 and almost all of us were still on summer vacation. We were getting older and becoming more independent minded, which tried our mother's patience. It was also a tough time for the nation, as there was rebellion, if not revolution, in the air. Our father warned us that, if we did not behave, there would be a heavy price to pay.

Our litmus test for defining who was behaving was simply divided into two areas. First, and most important, was to obey our mother. Second was to do well in school. The second area is easy to rationalize; it was a numbers game. Even social scientists, who studied birth order and intelligence, will argue that with sixteen children a few were bound to have scholastic lapses. However, this logic did not sit well with our father.

When we were growing up, report cards were dispersed right before Halloween—a cruel schedule, indeed. Our father warned (he was not one for idle threats) that if we got a bad report card, we were forbidden to go trick or treating—a harsh punishment for sure.

There were several Halloweens when one or more siblings were not allowed out for trick or treating due to a poor report card. To us it was cruel, and to the outside word, it was unusual; maybe far beyond corporal punishment. Given the number of children in our family, the bell curve would undoubtedly include some bottom feeders.

The other area mentioned—obey your mother—was even more important. Our father warned that if we did not improve our behavior, the whole family would have to stay in for Halloween. No biggie for the older siblings, but a nightmare for the young kids. And how would we explain this to our friends? We always thought someone should contact the Department of Family and Human Services for such punishment.

Lo and behold in the fall of 1967, we did not heed our father's warning. On the Sunday before Halloween, our father declared that we would be campused for Halloween night. Our only hope was that he may be stuck at the hospital, and we could go out for a few hours without him ever knowing. Not a chance. He came home extra early that day and started decorating the house for the trick-or-treaters, which we found to be preposterous. We wondered how could he think about accommodating the neighborhood trick-or-treaters when his own kids were sequestered.

When the first doorbell rang, our father and mother asked us to invite the trick-or-treaters in, while they went into the living room, dressed in simple, but disconcerting, costumes. They said nothing to the Halloween visitors, who seemed frightened by their antics. After a few acts like this, we decided this could be fun. So we stopped crying, and went to the basement to find a costume. Thus began our first Haunted House consisting of a cast of ghouls, goblins, witches, and all kinds of frightening creatures. The older siblings soon joined in, and we had enough talent to rival the local, commercial haunted houses. It was the best Halloween we ever had without even ringing a doorbell.

We vowed to help out the next year, and we kept that vow. We no longer went out on Halloween but stayed in to set up a haunted house. Each year the decorations became more sophisticated, and the cast grew with friends and relatives coming over to be part of the show. As time went by, the next generation of children took their places in the haunted house tradition.

Staying in character was mandatory while on the set. One warm Halloween we moved the set to the porch. This allowed for more talent to scare unsuspecting trick-or-treaters. We also learned that the eeriest part of the show was not the sophisticated props and other sights and sounds, but live actors dressed in scary costumes, who remained silent. Some say our tongues were tied, because we were scarred for life when we were not allowed out on Halloween night in '67.

Regardless, the night became a tradition in our neighborhood. Soon after school began in September, the kids in the neighborhood started to question each other if they would be brave enough to go to our house for Halloween. It soon became a rite of passage. Older kids came back during their high school years to prove they were no longer scared, but merely curious.

As years went by, we wondered how long we could keep the tradition going. A positive sign that the tradition would last was the continuing growth of the cast of characters joining our haunted crew. Each year there was always a surprise guest cast member. Siblings brought friends home from college, and cousins joined in the antics. What was most endearing was how the cast consisted of the eldest family members all the way down to the youngest. Bravery was the only prerequisite.

Our family Halloweens, even as youngsters, were not about roaming the streets but being part of a major happening in a neighborhood packed with children. This was a relief for the parents. They knew the kids were close by—simply out on the front porch or lawn having a ball on Halloween night. Hence, the adults in the neighborhood loved us.

Some years the cast was not more than four, but the lure of our haunted house was so compelling that nobody noticed if it was a lean cast year. For thirty-three years, our house was transformed to be the best house in the neighborhood on Halloween. This tradition was our father's gift to us, and the best Halloween treat ever. He put an unruly family to good use. From that night in 1967, we wished everyone a very special Halloween as part of our silent penance for misbehaving.

## YOU SHALL BE HOLY THE WHOLE WEEK.

Our family was schooled on the deep meaning of every holiday. Halloween was fun for sure, and everyone loved Christmas. And if it was a sanctioned holy day, we were shown how to keep it holy. Leaders of the Catholic Church traditionally view Easter as the paragon of our celebrated holidays and our parents, who were very pious, did not dispute it.

Our mother's piety went beyond her religious convictions. Yes, she often prayed the rosary and observed the holy days. But she also gained "saint" status once someone learned she was the mother of sixteen children. That was a fair assessment. But our evidence of her sainthood went beyond her prolific procreation.

Some mornings our mother would comment that she had a pleasant sleep in which she "dreamed of angels," something few people can claim. We witnessed her commitment to what she referred to as a "simple faith" in both obvious and subtle ways. She attended Mass every Sunday, as well as all holy days of obligation. She said Easter was her favorite holiday, as she "loved the services." When we were older and no longer needed to come home for lunch during school hours, she attended the noon mass during Lent. If there was cause for a "good excuse" not to observe something religious given her busy schedule, no one would judge her.

But she carried on, meeting all religious obligations.

Both our parents lived as true Christians. They never raised their voices to each other nor said a disparaging word about another person nor uttered an uncouth or uncivilized word. Such character, at least, gets you in the running for sainthood.

This quiet pious demeanor was not always the case. Our mother's religious devotions were not always subtle as she often spewed spirited words or phrases that gave her immediate relief to some mild annoyance or a more serious crisis. Some good examples include:

*Blessed Mother!* These two words were invoked liberally and used for minor incidents. There was no cause for concern.

*Blessed Hour!* These words were used for a longer incident and signaled to be on guard for what could unfold.

*Jesus, Mary, and Joseph.* Calling the trio was not taking their names in vain. This was used for external world events, such as the plight of a people, a natural disaster, or a war. This was her way of dealing with Weltschmerz.

*The Lord knows.* This was our mother's signal that you had one last chance to fess up, if she sensed you were fibbing.

*I cannot have one thing, not one blessed thing in this house.* This was declared when we broke something of hers, which was daily.

*Prayer to Saint Anthony for lost things.* While she shared this trick with us to use when we lost something relatively insignificant, our sense was she had no quota for how many times Anthony could be summoned by her, and no qualms about wanting an expedited response. With that many kids to manage, it was just not fair to lose stuff.

*Unsettling lighting and thunder.* Mother said there was no cause to worry. The angels were bowling up in the heavens. This was not comforting.

Priestly and religious orders often referred to our father as a saint. He did not have a conventional Catholic education upbringing; his early religious education consisted of home training by his mother and sporadic Sunday school until he was twelve years old. He attended public school in Philadelphia for twelve years and his subsequent education was mainly in the public education sector. As he explained, during this time period he "worshipped the Sacred Cow of Science." He was not even enamored by religion; it just wasn't that important to him.

Then his religious perspective changed. While preparing for his acceptance to medical school, he attended a faith-based university, which required taking religion courses. He had no special affinity for the content; he just wanted to get the required coursework done in order to proceed to medical school. Much to his surprise, these religion courses were an awakening for him. His curiosity was piqued, and he suddenly became interested in Jesus as he was presented in the mandatory theology courses. He felt a few prods from the Augustinian priests and brothers and believed these courses held a real epiphany for him. Like Zacchaeus, he climbed down the tree to get a better look at Catholic doctrine. He explained that his agnosticism was "really a convenient cop-out—a means of avoiding a commitment." He realized that, while he had excellent scholastic formation, he had, in reality, missed completely that "superb gift—a Catholic formation." He vowed that none of his children would miss so great an opportunity. So, Catholic formation for us was a given—lots of it.

Holy Week was observed the whole week at our house. On the evening of Palm Sunday, the beginning of Holy Week, our father would unveil his homemade Paschal candle. Catholics recognize the Paschal candle as an integral part of the Easter season. We had one in our dining room, meticulously decorated to Catholic worship standards on a specially made wooden stand. Each of us got to see our personally designated straight pin, which our father used to represent each of us, stuck in this tall, white candle, which represents Christ for Catholics. A new candle is used each year and is repurposed throughout the year for special occasions (e.g., baptisms, which filled most of the Sundays in our family). The candle was placed in the living room during the holidays.

On Palm Sunday, our father quizzed us on the history, the meaning and our family's use of the Pascal candle. One Sunday a friend, who was staying for dinner, asked if the pastor loaned out the Paschal candle to the families in the parish. We had to explain that it was our personal Paschal candle. "Wow!" he exclaimed. "You guys are, like, really serious Catholics."

We were definitely a serious Catholic family. Since most of us attended Catholic schools, we were let out on Wednesday of Holy Week for the Easter holiday. And even though Holy Thursday did not have mandatory services, we practiced several of our own.

We celebrated Christian Seder. Living in a neighborhood with many Jewish neighbors, we were familiar with Seder observances. This led us to wonder why we had to perform a Seder service. Wasn't that only for the Jewish families? We knew that Passover was an important Jewish feast that commemorated the redemption and liberation of the Israelites from their bondage in Egypt. For Catholics, Holy Thursday is the time to recall the Last Supper. Orthodox Catholics memorialize their Judeo-Christian roots by observing a type of Seder service, as well, on Holy Thursday night. This is a stretch for Catholics not only conceptually but also practically. Imagine our mother's angst having to prepare a major Seder service for the whole family when Easter Sunday was a few days away.

Consider the foods served at a Seder: Matzho, Maror (bitter herbs), Charoses (mixture of apples, nuts, and cinnamon), roasted egg, parsley, wine, and the big dish—lamb. These were not items readily available, and if so, they had to be prepared just right. Also keep in mind that many dishes were needed, which meant setting them up and then cleaning them. Again, all of this preparation and cleaning was done just a few days before Easter Sunday, when many people would be over for dinner. And the Easter dinner was no easy meal, as the Italians not only had fish and foul, but our mother prepared a three-layer lasagna.

Special prayer books were set on the table, which we read and read and read some more. One Seder tradition has the youngest son read the question, "Why is this night different from all the other nights." One of the older boys inevitably mumbled under his breath, "I can tell you why this night is different. All of our friends are hanging out tonight, and we are in here doing the stuff that the Jewish families do. I thought we were Catholics?" This did not escape our father's notice, so he doubled the readings for the service, kosher or not.

The meal provided some comic relief, as it was not clear who would get real wine and who got grape juice to symbolize the wine. Our father was not as acutely aware of everyone's age as our mother, thus the older kids wreaked havoc by switching receptacles around. The problem was that the small glasses were all the same, whether wine or grape juice was poured. The bigger concern was someone not used to wine getting giddy during a reading in which we risked suffering with more readings.

By the end of our Christian Seder, it was well into the evening. Our mother was exhausted, so the older ones, in good form, could not abandon her and go out with friends. There was much to clean up and prepare for additional baking on Good Friday. The older boys used a pass saying they had to get ready for the Thursday night "watch" at church when the Eucharist is taken to a side altar of repose after the Holy Thursday Mass of the Last Supper. Traditionally, the men of the parish (later women were involved) stood watch in solemn prayer, commemorating the apostles failing to stay up with Jesus when he was praying before Judas sold him to the Roman soldiers for captive. Thus, parishioners signed up for a one-hour watch at the Eucharist in repose in the church.

Given the Thursday evening activity, it was not easy to rise early on Friday morning. There is no Mass celebrated on Good Friday, although there may be readings and sermons by the pastor.

Catholics traditionally stay inside between noon and 3:00 p.m. in remembrance of Jesus' pain and suffering on the cross. Not only were we not allowed outside during this time, but our father would mimic the Holy Thursday night services at the church. He designed a homegrown adoration, taking advantage of his prayerful children. He placed a kneeler in his large study replete with prayer books. As a physician, he was quite conscious of safety, so we were asked to focus on an electric candle. Each child had to sign up for a half-hour of prayer on the kneeler. All lights were out except for the flickering light of the candle. When the heavy, sliding pocket door shut, it was judgment time. For us, this half hour seemed like an eternity, yet nobody dared to move from the kneeler. Later, we compared notes on how we survived. The most popular diversion was to consider what to do with the eyes (i.e., open/closed; one open, wandering or starring).

By Friday evening we had about thirty-six hours of sequester. Our father asked who wanted to go visit the churches, specifically the Eucharist in repose, which was a tradition on Holy Thursday evening. Since we were commemorating the Passover that night, we missed this opportunity— so we thought. The chance to get out was compelling, so we loaded the station wagon and gave our requests to our father on which churches to visit. However, he had other ideas. He knew which were the most ornate churches in the area.

The evening was kind of neat. We parked the car in the church lot while our father explained that we must be solemn and quiet, especially since this was not our parish, and the congregations may not be used to a throng of children storming the altar, which is exactly what we did. It became a race from the parking lot to the foot of the altar. A dozen kids ran up the aisles. It was not clear if saying the prayer before the Eucharist was part of the race. Regardless, local parishioners were impressed with a group of children being eager to pray; little did they know this was part of our furlough. When we reassembled in the car, we asked which church was next. On the way to the next church we compared the one we left with others. By the end of the night, we each said which was the "best church" to visit for style and presentation.

The Saturday before Easter Sunday was naturally dedicated to preparations, which were mostly cleaning. In our house, a good cleaning took time. The main rooms to be cleaned were the living room, dining room, and master bedroom, since the common areas were cleaned regularly. This required dusting, mopping and vacuuming.

One benefit to cleaning was playing music. Whoever was in charge of a room chose the albums to play or what radio station to listen to. It made the chore move much faster.

Food preparation began early in the morning. We dared not to venture into the kitchen lest we got a job. When a mass of people gathered in the kitchen, our mother announced, "Whoever does not have a function in this kitchen get out, otherwise you are getting a job to do." That was enough to clear the area.

Back in those days, patients sent our father, a physician, gifts during the holidays. Christmas and Easter were occasions for all types of food. We had baskets, bushels, and sometimes crates of fruit, from which our mother made a healthy fruit cup as the first course of the Easter meal. We received vegetable trays from which our mother organized a major antipasto salad—a real Italian antipasto. There would be a turkey or ham, but the major part of the meal would be the three-layer lasagna.

Preparation for the lasagna began Saturday and required all tables in the kitchen. Our mother used extra thick, flat noodles that were cooked in a big pot. The red sauce (or gravy) took up another range. (Good thing we had a six-range stove.) There was also plenty of ricotta cheese.

The most fun was looking for the special desserts, which consisted of Easter bread, Easter pie (ricotta pie), pizelles, cannolis, cookies, and boxes of chocolates with nuts and jellies.

In the early afternoon on Saturday, each child was summoned to his or her room for a final inspection of what would be worn for Easter Sunday mass. The older siblings helped the younger ones. Our grandmother may have made a dress or suit for some of us. In those cases a delegation was sent to the room, and the child needed to be fully dressed to go downstairs to model the new outfit. Invariably there were complaints from the girls that the dresses hung too low from the knees, and the boys grumbled that the pants were cuffed too high. Given that both grandparents were tailors, their judge of what was in style trumped our opinions every time.

As the early evening hours arrived, discussion began about who would attend the midnight mass. Even though our mother loved Easter services, especially midnight mass, the pressure was on to make sure all the food (and everything else) was ready. For us, there were pros and cons to going to midnight mass. If she went to midnight church services, the next morning could be more manageable for the thirty or more people to be served. Keeping the younger children up would mean they would sleep in the following morning. However, after a long hard day of work in the kitchen, cajoling the older children to finish the cleaning in the house and inspecting what was supposed to be done, it was difficult for her to catch a second wind. So, our mother's pat answer to "Are we going to midnight mass?" was "We'll have to see."

Our father never opted for the midnight mass. While he liked the idea that the church would be packed for a moving Easter Vigil, he knew it would be difficult to get the whole family together in a couple of pews.

Every kid loves an Easter egg hunt. We had a special one. First, our parents were not about to make up a dozen or so Easter baskets every year. So, our mother instituted making a massive Easter candy basket replete with jelly beans, marshmallow bunnies, chocolate crosses, and small coconut eggs. While it sat in the middle of the dining room table, it was never clear when the candy could be eaten. The big treat was our very own two-piece, milk chocolate egg in which we could hold other candy.

The hunt experience for finding our own Easter egg depended upon age. Hiding the youngest kids' eggs was easy. Hide it in a place to make it interesting, but not too hard to have the sibling crying. To avoid such risk, we simply left those eggs for our father to hide. The middle kids had it the hardest. The older kids were allowed to hide these eggs; therefore, anything goes. They reveled in having us spend the morning hunting for the eggs. A middle kid is young enough to be interested in having a chocolate egg from which you could get more candy stored, but old enough to not cry foul to the parents if unable to find the egg that the older siblings hid.

The older kids got an egg nominally, but several donated theirs to the main basket or gave it to a younger sibling to break out late spring. An added variable was that with so many eggs "on the street," we could easily stumble onto someone else's egg. It was verboten to take an egg with another's name on it. But an unorthodox and unsanctioned practice occurred whereby if another person's egg was found, the finder would transfer it to another—usually much more difficult—place.

If the older sibling took mercy on the younger kid who vowed to "give up" on the hunt, he or she went to fetch the egg from where it was cleverly hidden. Unfortunately in most cases, it was gone. The one who appropriated the egg would not fess up, claiming paybacks from a prior year of emotional duress when it was done to him or her. There was really no one to adjudicate the Easter egg hunt shenanigans, and we dared not to bother our mother with such a mundane problem especially when she felt the pressure of entertaining a small battalion for Easter dinner. Nor would we dare to complain to our father as he would retell the Passion story, and ask if not finding your egg was really a serious matter.

If we were lucky to find our egg that year, there was still a challenge. Our father filled our "hallow eggs" with other candy, if we answered his questions correctly. These were not warm and fuzzy questions about Peter Cottontail. These were hard-core questions about the Passion, historical Jesus, Catholic symbolism, and even theology. Before you got a question, our father conducted his mini history and physical to judge the level of difficulty, such as how old are you, what grade are you in, what are you studying in religion class, etc.

But we learned there was only one level to his questions—difficult. Consider these for example: What were the seven sayings that Jesus Christ uttered while he was hanging on the cross? Name the five sorrowful mysteries in order. Explain the transfiguration. What was the number of Roman soldier whips sanctioned to criminals during the time of Jesus' crucifixion? What was the inscription on top of the crucifix and what does it mean? What was telling of the Biblical report "…and out poured water and blood" after Jesus was stabbed by a Roman lance? Needless to say, the candy fill line did not move quickly.

After all of the cleaning and praying during Holy Week, we thought we deserved to be in the Diaconate or the Third Order of Franciscans or Third Order of Carmelites or third order of something. This gave us the sense that we were not the run-of-the-mill Catholics. One year, one of the older boys thought he would be smart and lay prostrate in the Easter candy line to get psyched for the questions. When asked by our father what he was doing, he said he was "praying by prostate." Being a gastrointestinal physician, our father laughed. However, that trick bought him a week's stay with the Trinity Missionaries during the summer.

Oddly, we did not have anyone join a religious order, but it was not from lack of trying by our father. He brought new meaning to the strategy of "soft sell" to begin discernment to the priesthood or a religious sisters' order. His proactive steps were much more than the sending us to an occasional day or weekend retreat.

One summer, one brother was told to pack a suitcase under the misconception that he going to the seashore. He was given $5 and endured a nine-hour bus trip to the headquarters of a foreign missionary order. He had no idea where he was going and why. Upon arrival, he was introduced to a group of young men called "Brothers." There must have been 100 boys between the ages of 12 and 15 in attendance, some having accents our brother did not recognize. It was un-Godly hot but a beautiful place in which the grass was greener than any major league baseball field.

The boys were placed into groups. The first order of business was to turn over all of their personal belongings, mostly money. They were told that they could retrieve their money at the canteen run by Brother Terry. Our brother only had a few dollars left since he spent some of it at the turnpike rest stops. Most of the boys had $20 and even $50. Next, the campers were asked to write a letter to their parents telling them that they had arrived safely.

Throughout the week, our brother went to the canteen for a soda or candy bar. Odd thing, though, the Brother supervisor never mentioned that his account was empty by Tuesday. Unbeknownst to our brother, the good Brothers put him on scholarship, something he never forgot.

The week was tremendous. While classes were held about things he couldn't recall, there was plenty of time for fun things such as swimming and volleyball. Mass was said every evening on a grassy knoll. The boys slept in small cots assembled in a large room. It was so hot they did not need covers.

## BLESSED BE THY HOUSE.

Our house was decorated with religious relics similar to how a house would be decorated for Christmas. Families, even strict Catholic families, don't deck the halls for Easter. But we did. Yet Easter decorating was easy since most of the items were up year round. These were not the common Easter bunnies and Easter eggs but serious religious articles. At some level, our father was furnishing a church, even to the exhaustion of our mother. We had pews in the home and kneelers for serious meditation. When new carpeting was put in the front staircase, the installer asked our mother how many priests and nuns were part of her sixteen children.

The front staircase wall was dedicated to the Blessed Mother and comprised of fifteen paintings or some type of sculpture. At the first landing, there was as a marble Pieta. Around the corner near the final few steps approaching the second floor hallway wall, hung a very graphic painting of the crucifixion with the two Mary's at the foot of the cross. There were also framed pictures of all fourteen Stations of the Cross on our second floor hallway. In the third floor hallway hung a wooden crucifix, which could have been set in a small chapel.

Each of our bedrooms required a crucifix. Nightlights created another opportunity for religious article luminaries. Our parents' bedroom had the Madonna and child painting above their bed. A very colorful and scary wooden bust of Christ with thorns on his head was on our father's chest-of-drawers, along with a wooden statue of St. Joseph holding the Christ child. Another Pieta adorned a windowsill.

A sundry of religious statues and paintings, such as St. John Neumann, Mother Katherine Drexel, and St. Francis of Assisi, were showcased around our home, which was a common practice for Italian and Philadelphian families. Any wall or ledge posed an opportunity to revere something religious.

As with most homes, the dining room was formal. There was little wall space for hanging paintings. We had Hans Holbein's 16th century rendition of St. Thomas More, the English statesman and counsel who became the Catholic patron of lawyers and jurists. It set the tone for the room, where some serious dialogue took place. Even the basement billiard room had religious articles including a very graphic crucifixion affixed near the billiards break. Our older brothers told us that served as a reminder to those who considered cheating in the game.

The spacious property outside was another opportunity for religious displays. A Sacred Heart of Jesus stone statue set on a large cement lift, and a colorful fiberglass canapé (that matched the red color of the Sacred Heart) greeted family and visitors as they drove up the meandering driveway. Being of Italian descent, we also had a grotto. But our grotto was the size of the foundation of a small chapel. It required a team of bricklayers, who could have passed for the Army Corps of Engineers, to install it. It consisted of cement pews, inlaid religious symbols on the floor, and knee-high brick walls to place religious statues that were worthy of being in any major church. Each was encased in some type of hut to protect it from the weather.

Our father always wanted a gazebo. Just before he died, the carpenters in our extended family finally finished an octagon-shaped gazebo that measured twenty-two feet across and peeked at twenty-two feet from the ground. It had seating all around and extra wide steps from the back. The most remarkable part was not the wood or the ornate design, but the eight stained-glass panels inscribed with a religious symbol: There was the alpha and the omega and A.M.D.G. (Latin acronym "For the greater glory of God.)

As if this glorification were not enough, our father once considered buying the convent owned by a local parish. He thought it would be quite convenient to go to daily mass in the convent's chapel, which could be presided over by one of the priests who could walk across the lawn. When we discovered it had fifteen bedrooms, it didn't seem as crazy as it appeared. With that many bedrooms we could each have our own sanctuary.

**WE GIVE THEE THANKS.**

Over the river and through the woods to grandmother's house we did not go…Grandmother and grandfather, on both sides of our family, came to our house. Interesting, even though they had other children who lived in less-crowded homes, they came to our home. What's Thanksgiving without grandparents, right?

As William Shakespeare said, "There is history in all men's lives." Thanksgiving seemed to be a good time to learn about our history. From the moment our grandparents arrived to the time they left, someone was always vying for their attention. We were well aware that there was little novelty to being a grandchild of theirs, as they had many others. However, true to human nature, there was competition to be grandmother's favorite. Bragging rights were at stake.

Our father's mother had a very reasonable response when asked by a grandchild if he or she was "the favorite." She showed us her hand and pointed to a finger and said, "If you cut this finger, I bleed and hurt. If you cut this finger (pointing to another finger), I bleed and hurt." Good answer.

Our maternal grandmother had a different strategy. She gave the allusion that each of us were at least among the favored few. This gave both her and the grandchild some satisfaction without answering the delicate question.

Similar to Easter and Christmas, the main stage for the Thanksgiving dinner was the dining room. This was a formal dining area, in which lights were rarely on. It had a large, arched entryway (no door) from a formal foyer and a swinging door entryway to the kitchen that made service "easy," assuming you had some type of servant (which we did not). There was a servant's buzzer on the floor at one end of the table. As kids, we enjoyed climbing under the table and pressing the buzzer until our mother "had enough," and one of the older children reprimanded the ones disturbing the peace.

The dining room was impressive with several breakfronts, a mirror that took up half a wall, a china cabinet almost to the ceiling, and candelabras with decorative crystal hangings around the room. Besides the aforementioned Saint Thomas More painting, there was a huge table that could have outdistanced the room, if all the leaves were inserted. The table comfortably fit twenty people, but there was always the need to squeeze more, as one child always made claim that he or she was now "big enough" to sit in this main dining area and "not have to eat with the little kids at the other two kitchen tables."

Thanksgiving had three tables set and the obligatory four-seat card table that probably every American family had. Our mother had difficulty finding a table cloth big enough, so she bought two of the same kind and had our grandmother, the seamstress, sew them together. There were two colors: red for Christmas, and gold for Easter and Thanksgiving. The table was placed on a large oriental rug that never lost its luster. There were two six-post silver candelabras and complete sets of silver servings on top of the several breakfronts.

Getting dishes out of the breakfronts was a major event. Our mother recruited two people, one to retrieve the dishes set low in these units, and one to carry the dishes to the various tables. She gave the orders accompanied by brief histories about all the wares in the room. Our mother explained that since she lived for so many years with her in-laws, she really did not have time to use her fancy dinnerware, and by the time the children were old enough to enjoy a fancy table display, she did not have enough place settings, given that twelve seemed to be the maximum secured by any style. All of these wares were stylish but always functional. But what it meant to us was there was more to clean.

Our father was an eclectic man with many interests, professionally and personally, but rarely assisted in domestic projects. One Thanksgiving, he called our mother very excited. He knew there would be a lot of people for Thanksgiving, so he procured a thirty-five-pound turkey. Our mother explained that it was true that we had a big oven (six ranges with a side oven), but it would not fit a thirty-five-pound turkey, and the time it would take to cook, even if it fit, would have been starting on Halloween. She explained the fifteen-minutes per pound rule, and given that our father was a gastrointestinal doctor, it is best to be risk averse with food served to many people. Solution? Our father explained the problem to the Franciscan sisters at the hospital. One sister said that they would simply have it cooked in the hospital's kitchen. Problem solved.

## FRIENDS IN HIGH PLACES

Having a lot of priests, brothers, and nuns as friends, acquaintances, or professional colleagues had interesting rewards. Our father had many with several friends in high places. He was the Archdiocesan cardinal's personal physician, and yes, he made house calls to the cardinal's home.

Periodically, the cardinal asked our father to bring our mother and "some of the children" for dinner. For most people, this would be an honor and filled with excitement. For our mother—our poor mother—this was high anxiety. She not only had to ready the group but pray that nothing would "come from the mouths of babes" to embarrass her.

The cardinal was always welcoming and his resident's formal dining table was the only table we knew that rivaled ours (but ours was still bigger). We rehearsed how the cardinal should be addressed and discussed at length why we would kiss his ring.

There was always a "first claim" for who would ring the doorbell and be greeted by a woman, who was one of a small group of sisters that tended to the house and gave domestic support to the cardinal, his staff, dignitaries, and visitors. Not sure which category we fit; we asked our mother if we qualified as dignitaries. She explained that the cardinal was very pleased to see his doctor's family, but as far as she was concerned she prayed that the visit be unremarkable. As we got older, we learned what that meant.

Once inside, we were escorted to what was one of several living rooms, replete with more furniture than a museum. A few words of welcome were exchanged, and then our father and the cardinal disappeared for doctor/patient confidentiality matters. Our mother assured us that the cardinal was not sick, but that this was simply a checkup visit. One of the younger kids asked why the cardinal did not go to our father's office in South Philadelphia. Another explained that bishops and popes do not know how to drive while another sibling denied that. This brought on much banter among us about what temporal matters cardinals were able to do, given that they received assistance, such as holding their "cane" and "taking off their hats and stuff."

Invariably, musical chairs ensued, since we wanted to try out every chair and sofa. We knew not to sit on any chair that had a sash around the seat even though it was tempting. One sibling said the chair was broken; another said someone important sat there and once that happens nobody else is allowed to sit in the chair. An older sibling helped our mother by asking, "Are you kids going to say such stupid things when we eat dinner with the cardinal and embarrass your mother and father?" Our mother appreciated the help but warned that "stupid" was not a nice word.

With all the hopping up and down on the furniture, shoes became untied, shirttails dropped, and dresses became less "lady like." Mother was in overdrive yet got each child fixed in a second. It never seemed a long period of time since our father and the cardinal slipped away, because there were so many things to see and discuss. But it must have felt like an eternity for our mother.

A louder than normal pronouncement came from the cardinal when he returned and said, "So, shall we eat?" There was never a dissenting opinion.

The cardinal did not sit "at the head of the table," but rather in the middle. He explained that this gave him better range to speak and hear *a destra* or *a sinistra* (to the right or to the left). Later, our mother adopted this at our home, even though we know our father secretly did not like the new seating arrangements. We missed seeing him deep at the end of the long dining room table against the backdrop of three handsome windows that bowed around that side of the room where the lighting began to fade.

We took our seats at the cardinal's table in a natural order. The younger ones sat closest to our mother, and the older ones got as far from the cardinal as they could, fearing they would be asked questions more challenging than our father's Easter Sunday quizzes.

The grace before meals was actually shorter than ours. Who would think we had bragging rights over the length of a cardinal's dinner prayers? A highlight was when the cardinal rang a small bell to alert the sisters in-residence to come from the kitchen to the dining room. (We never did see that kitchen, even though our mother would have loved to see it but never dared to ask.) He would let one of the younger ones ring the bell. They got a charge out of this, especially when they rang the bell for no real need, and the sister giggled politely.

The cardinal was a tall man with large features. His voice was soft, and he spoke ever so slowly. One occasion while we were readying to accompany our father to the cardinal's home, our younger brother, a conscientious objector, confronted our father and announced he had enough of the cardinal visits. When asked why he did not want to go, he merely said, "He takes too long to ask questions and even longer to answer mine."

Over time we learned that he would ask questions about more mundane matters, rather than higher order theology. He asked about which school we attended, and being that we all were at Catholic schools, he gave a brief history of the religious order that ran the school. Eventually, we were schooled on the history of Sisters of Mercy, Augustinians, Christian Brothers, and the Jesuits. He had a closing remark about the Jesuits that only he and our parents understood and laughed about. Maybe that is why many of us went to Jesuit colleges—to figure out the joke.

Oddly enough, we were not so impressed with the food at the table even though we were pleased with the food the cardinal sent at the holidays. We are not talking about simple baskets of fruit; rather, we received crates of fruit and all sorts of what we considered exotic food. This was a conversation that our mother would be most active in, as she would run interference to defend the cardinal. We did not understand that he would not know what was sent in particular, just that something nice was sent.

The head sister would sometimes sit with us for coffee and dessert. She asked our mother who helped her cook and serve the scores of people coming for the high holidays, assuming outside help came to assist. Our mother used this as an opportunity to explain that everyone pitches in, plus she gets a lot of help from her mother-in-law. It made sense, given our paternal grandmother emigrated from Italy and knew plenty about cooking. She explained how well they worked together in the kitchen, and how they knew each other's moves and played to each other's strengths. The sister agreed that a lot of help and good organization of responsibilities was required to run things smoothly in a kitchen. The cardinal would interject and offered our mother services of the sisters if things got too challenging. Our mother winked at the sister and replied that she would send over the directions to our house.

The dinner party ended when our mother dropped her head and asked the cardinal to bless the family (we all did the same). On one occasion as we exited through the front door, one of the boys noticed at least four metro Sunday newspapers placed on a large table just inside the doorway. He asked the cardinal's personal secretary if the cardinal read all of these newspapers. He replied, "Every page." Given we knew the cardinal to be a smart man, we learned that reading a metro newspaper everyday was a good habit of industry.

Leaving the cardinal's residence through the gate, our mother commented on the size of the home and how neat it would be to live there. One of the older girls yelled, "Yes, but I would not want to clean it." A young sibling asked if next time we were invited, would we be able to sleep over.

Fortunately, all the visits to the cardinal's residence went without incident; our mother gave thanks on the ride home. While it was nice to get invited somewhere, these trips were understandably stressful each time for her.

Once around Christmas, the cardinal's personal chauffeur dropped off the goods and exposed the gifting strategy. We essentially got what the cardinal had in excess. It was fine with him as it made his selection for what to drop off easier.

Cardinals (and bishops) confirm Catholics around the fifth or sixth grade. One Confirmation, we discovered that the cardinal would be presiding. Our mother reminded the confirmand that the cardinal had recently sent over a delicious crate of Florida oranges. Therefore, someone recommended that he began rehearsing how to slip in a grand "Thank you" before the slap on the check. Our mother's feeling about this overture—one we heard often—was, "Don't you dare."

## AWAY IN A MANGER...

The notion of Christmas in July just never made sense to our mother. It was not the cognitive dissonance thinking about Christmas when it was "hotter than July." The calendar really gave her no reprieve for what needed to get done in these big families. Half of the children's birthdays fell between mid-November and the end of the year, as well as the New Year's Eve celebration.

Our mother said she needed to get into the Christmas spirit, and she didn't enjoy Christmas shopping outside the season. Even when we were old enough to know that Santa Claus was more of a symbol of the joyous season, our mother managed to maintain the Christmas mystique. For example, there were three fundamental questions we had about Christmas, for which she was not forthcoming of answers: Where is the shopping list; when is the shopping taking place; and where are all of the gifts stored for the good little children? Our mother was a master of discretion, so it was easy for her to keep a secret.

Christmas was a real transformation in our home, and there was no "getting started early." You were not allowed to "put things up" until our mother gave the ok to move masses of materials from the deep, back recesses of the basement to the first floor. She never panicked about being ready for Christmas. She knew this was a high-stakes occasion for us, which meant we were willing servants to appease every wish in the hopes of possibly gathering some intelligence for what could appear on Christmas morning.

When our mother's "right time" arrived, we went to the basement to fulfill the mission. Box after box was taken upstairs and placed in the room that housed the decorations. Our mother determined teams with a directive such as "You! You and your sister kindly take this box and set up [this, that, or the other thing]."

The most favored decorations were the mangers (inside and out). Setting up the inside manger was not too much trouble; the challenge started in trying to guess which manger set our father favored that year, plus keeping at bay and in the basement those manger sets that had broken pieces. Broken pieces were never fixed, and the sets were never discarded. Our father simply added another set commandeered by some religious associate. Consequently, we had three to four manger sets spread out on the foyer floor, waiting for one to be placed inside the big fireplace.

We experimented with several iterations of manger set-ups. "Just put one up, they won't make us take it down," was our rationale. Well, they did. "They will never know these pieces don't match." They knew. We wondered how they expected us to know which manger set was the most recent one. These rhetorical questions did not go over well. If you were not up for the task, you were simply re-assigned to a less prestigious duty that had something to do with glue and glitter.

Our manger sets were all-inclusive sets, no abridged versions. We made a game out of guessing the pieces as we unwrapped them. One camel was a dead give-away, because of its size; but the "lazy camel," as we called him, was sitting down and about the size of another animal standing. Piece-by-piece, each team unwrapped the manger pieces. Before we knew it, the operation drew a crowd.

Plenty of advice was provided to the workers by those assembled. There was the constant reminder as each piece was unwrapped. "Don't break the piece," since we were fearful that a broken piece would result in another manger set into the house.

The prize piece was the baby Jesus, which was not easily found given its small size. Those siblings, who put the manger away the previous year, felt the pressure. What if it was lost? What if they broke it and neglected to tell anyone? The only advantage to replacing the statue was we knew we had time, since the baby Jesus was not put into the manger until Christmas morning. What a relief when it was found.

The final piece we hung was the angel. The height placement had to be just right, as this was the first piece inspected by our mother. There was no easy way to hang it, and needless to say, our family produced no burgeoning engineers. If it slipped while hanging, it would surely break.

When all the pieces were found, the fine-tuning took place. Mary and Joseph were easy, but after that there was variance of opinions of who goes on the right side and who goes on the left side, i.e., shepherds versus wise men. Then came the question of how far apart each piece was to another, and where to place the animals that "must have stunk the place out." When the team was satisfied, someone called for our mother to inspect our work. She entered, put all the lights on, and said, "Let's see." Most families talk about the prize turkey or prize pudding that has to be just right at Christmas. For our family, it was the manger display. And this was just the inside one.

Each neighborhood has marquee decorations that the residents bank on to get them into the Christmas spirit. Ours was the manger set on our front lawn. Putting up the outside manger was a battle. Many of the little kids were willing to help, but there was not much for them to do. Hauling life-size, cement statues of figures for a manger that were big enough for a cathedral, did not enamor the older boys. Another task was setting up the handmade stable, which was made by one of our father's patients, who was a carpenter. It was massive, close to being the size of a small row home in south Philly. The assemblage, which included a large, one-piece roof, had to be dug out of the garage and carried to the front lawn. Invariably, it was always cold or raining and sometimes both.

Industrial-size, heavy bolts held the pieces together. Configuring the outside assembling process of where each piece went and how far apart they stood from each other was similar to the inside manger set up. At some point during the construction, our father would arrive home from work, park his car half way up the driveway and step out to make an adjustment. His first look was at the positioning of the two spotlights. The large white star could not simply hang behind the manger on a bush. No such luck. We had to climb the tree behind the manger and place the star high, high up so that it was the highest star set in the neighborhood.

On Christmas Eve, our father sent the oldest boy and a posse to get reduced-priced Christmas trees to set beside the manger. It was one of the few times that one of the children was allowed to drive our mother's station wagon. Four Christmas trees were placed beside this manger.

Decorating the rest of the outside with lights soon became a competition to see who could place a string of lights the highest on a huge Chinese cherry blossom tree.

As with many competitions, it becomes more interesting with bodily risk; and there was risk involved in stringing lights around the branches of a tree that reached several stories high. Each capable brother took his best shot. When the competition was complete, the tree looked like an octopus ride on the Jersey Shore boardwalk. On several occasions, the branches were too thin to climb, so we had to cut the lights. We suspect one brother threw the remaining few feet of lights, which was a violation. On another occasion, one brother recruited an assistant who leaned out a second floor window for a hand off in an effort to string the branches from that vantage point. Another violation.

Those of us who were risk averse stayed on the ground but created our own spectacle. One year, an older sister set strings of lights along the front lawn that rivaled a landing runway for the Philadelphia International Airport.

## GIFT GIVING

There were several years when we bought a Christmas gift for each other in addition to our parents and grandmother. The fun began just after school started in the fall, when we began our Christmas savings plan. A good bank was a large Tootsie Roll® carrier, but some siblings used the tried and true sock.

Our father knew the owner of the five-and-dime store across from the hospital where he worked. He brought us to the store about two hours before closing, so we could shop at once and knock out the scores of gifts. We were set up in teams with the older ones helping the younger siblings. We each took hand-held baskets and were careful not to bump into another sibling, who might peek into another basket. Around the store we went looking for something special or creative. Good thing the older ones were with us, as special and creative meant much more than we had saved since the summer. We loaded up on paper clip boxes, cool-looking pencil sharpeners, and a host of other functional items. Anything frivolous was a no-no.

Buying for our grandmother was easy. She received the obligatory bath powder or hard candy or liquorice candy, which is what we called "Grannie candy." She must have accumulated tons of it over the years. Our father got his share of aftershave. Picking out a gift for our mother was the first time we understood the expression, "It's the thought that counts."

The pace picked up as our two-hour shopping time limit went quickly. The purchase deal involved turning over our savings to one of the older siblings who then turned it over to our father, who paid the cashiers. Amazing, each year we had just enough money to cover the twenty or more Christmas gifts apiece. We knew we were great at Christmas shopping, but not that good. Our parents did double duty when it came to bringing the Christmas magic.

Trimming the tree took place either Christmas Eve or the day before the eve—no sooner. And since our father was big on risk management, the tree had to be safely and properly secured, which took half a day. At one level, trimming the tree was as quick as smashing a Piñata at a kid's birthday part—a couple of sweeps and it was done. With so many hands to contribute, the tree was quickly decorated, but not necessarily in good order. This occurred under our father's supervision. He was very sensitive to not hurting the little ones' feelings. So if some tinsel fell to the floor, it stayed on the floor. If tinsel was on the tree in globs, it stayed in globs.

Once the tree decorating was completed, someone summoned our mother to take a look. We plugged the tree lights in and turned out the room lights. When our mother came in, she turned on the room lights and said, "Let's see," then remarked, "The tree is beautiful." Is this the same women who asked for minuscule adjustments to the inside manger? Later in the evening our father rounded up a few of the creative older children and they did significant fine-tuning of the tree decorations. The little kids never questioned the difference on Christmas Day.

Hanging the children's stockings was harder than what Hollywood star got top billing on a theater's marquee. There was not enough room on the mantel to string sixteen stockings, let alone our parents' and grandmother's. Some had to double up. Objectors to doubling up were not related to age: Some older siblings could care less, while some younger ones were precocious enough not to have their stocking eclipsed by another sibling's stocking. They wanted their names in full view. Therefore, tough decisions had to be made by the two hanging the stockings. (We always worked in twos, so it was good our parents had an even number of children.)

The twins were easy, since they were used to buddying up. The alignment could not be changed from the birth order. This meant a few rounds of rock-paper-scissors to see whose stockings were placed in the front position. Given the stockings were hung on Christmas Eve, the stakes were too high to argue and cause a fuss. But during the rest of the season, the names on the stockings changed often. One of the older sisters always took the lead on hanging stockings. If you wanted a change, you had to see her. Yet changes rarely took place; she had an off-the-shelf rationale for where any decoration would go in the house.

Getting children to bed the night before Christmas was no problem. Our parents managed to do the Santa Claus tradition as well as any other parent. Even though they must have been exhausted by December 24, the nocturnal interruption started before Christmas morning with several stowaways in their bed. When we were little, it was fair game to bed hop, and the best bed hop was with our parents or at least with our father. Our mother was not a believer in having children in her bed; her sleep was precious. Our father, on the other hand, had no problem with a stowaway child.

The strategy for the children was to get the prime spot, which was on the outer side of our father, unseen and untouched by our mother. The next best spot was at the foot of the bed on our father's side. The other two slots were risky as they could encroach on our mother's side, but on

Christmas Eve we went for broke. Some Christmas mornings there were as many as four children in their bed.

When morning finally arrived, the children were naturally excited to go downstairs to see what Santa Claus brought. But we were not a family who allowed the kids to wake up and run downstairs to see what Santa left. In our house the gifts were placed in the living room in which the entryway had a huge sheet draped to block the view of what was inside. Inscribed on the sheet were several directives, such as "Do not open until Christmas" and "No peeking," as well as a Christmas tree and a bone cross skull drawn on the sheet. There were several tiny peep holes for which nobody claimed credit. If we really wanted to cheat, we stuck our head under the sheet for a quick look. This created a lot of excitement and lure in the early morning. Those who peeked denied it, while others were forthcoming with what they saw.

Our Christmas morning ritual began with the younger siblings waking up the older ones then assembling in our parents' room. Our parents' first order of business was to have a healthy cup of coffee. Several kids darted for the kitchen to be of service to these wonderful parents who made Christmas magical. We were also required to get coffee for the older siblings, as they threatened a slowdown to getting themselves together for the trip downstairs. The younger children never understood how these siblings were focused on getting their first hit of java while we were as excited as can be.

Once everyone was present, we lined up according to birth order from youngest to oldest. We had a tradition that each child got a turn at carrying baby Jesus down the stairs and placing him in the manger. We paraded down the stairs while singing a Christmas religious carol. Before the manger, we recited a few prayers.

Finally it was time to take down the sheet and proceed into the living room to see what Santa brought us. In the room were neat piles of unwrapped gifts. Given the children were so close in age, it was not immediately clear whose pile was whose, unless Santa brought a unique gift that the child was asking for since Thanksgiving. Our mother was quick to direct each child to the correct pile. After we accounted for our gifts, we went to see what the others got for Christmas. It was just as fun to do this. Our father sat in a recliner and observed the excitement.

In all the years I never heard a sibling say, "I did not get what I asked for." Our mother had a station wagon, not a sleigh. The wagon must have held many bags on her many Christmas shopping trips. We never saw any "elves" helping her. The adage "Some people pursue happiness; others create it" was written for her.

## HAPPY NEW YEAR

It truly was a Christmas season in our home, not simply a one- or two-day affair. Our parents made a special effort to visit their siblings the week between Christmas and New Year's, and we enjoyed seeing the aunts and uncles, including great aunts and uncles, and many cousins.

Occasionally, a few of us got to stay for dinner at a relative's house, since many of them had big families as well and knew how to accommodate large gatherings. It was neat to see the interaction during these visits—almost like looking into a mirror. It is then that we could observe the dynamics of a large family as others viewed our family. We discovered that the multiplicity of everyday events was truly remarkable in these big families. But as our mother always said, "A family is a family whether there is one child or sixteen."

When leaving a relative's home, our mother always extended a warm invitation to a big highlight of the Christmas season in our house—the New Year's Eve party. "You must come to our New Year's Eve party. Everyone will be there."

The New Year's party was always at our home. Rather than subject a sitter—even a family member—to handle a large number of children on what could be an explosive ring into the New Year, our parents thought it best to host the New Year's celebrations, a tradition that continued for their entire lives.

This tradition gave way to another tradition instituted by our father: Nobody goes out on New Year's Eve; everyone must attend the family party. While we didn't mind attending the family party when we were younger, we were not happy campers when we entered adolescence and young adulthood. At that age, there appeared to be better parties outside the home. But we soon discovered we were wrong. We had the best New Year's Eve parties. And while the rule of nobody goes out seemed restrictive, we could invite our friends. As our mother said, "Everyone will be there."

Invariably some relative or friend arrived at our house well after midnight claiming they had a lousy time at another New Year's celebration. They came knowing our family always had a warm and friendly New Year's party.

Just a few days before New Year's, the lobbying started among the kids to vie for staying up to midnight and being a part of the festivities. Becoming part of the party was an evolution, a right of initiation in our house. Each stage of the party participation offered some interesting times and memories. At one stage, we were permitted to stay up to 9:00 or 10:00 p.m.; as we got older, we stayed up long enough to hear the New Year's well wishing downstairs. Eventually, we graduated to dressing up and staying up until midnight then sent to our rooms for bed. The stages worked their way around the clock until the final stage in which we stayed up all night then went to church for the early morning mass. After church, we went to the Mummers Parade in South Philadelphia. If the weather was too cold, we watched it on television for hours on end.

The evolution process continued with the next generation. As young parents, we arrived early then left before midnight. As our children, nieces and nephews grew older, our families stayed later. Yet what remained the same was that our parents hosted the New Year's Eve party, a tradition they held from the year they bought their first house until the year they died. And every child attended the party every year; none of us knew a New Year's outside the homestead.

Preparations were very similar to any big event held at our home throughout the year. Yet, while the holidays were filled with good food and good cheer, there was a price to pay: cleaning and more cleaning; dusting and more dusting; shopping and more shopping; and decorating everything just right. Every fixture in the home seemed to grow in stature as a holiday approached—more windows, more blinds, more floors, more carpeting, more steps, more landings, and overall more furnishings everywhere. Lucky for our parents, they had a built-in team of servants, which had a pecking order for jobs.

In our father's terms, everything would "get the white glove test" and must be spic and span clean. A favorite cleaning was waxing the linoleum kitchen floor, since the kitchen played a central part of the party for several reasons including the dancing room once the tables were removed.

The process began when one of our older brothers went into the basement and retrieved an industrial-size floor buffer, which was apparently a hand-me-down from a hospital. This process was the trigger for the younger children to run upstairs and don a pair of thick socks.

Anxiously, they waited on the back steps every so often asking, "Mark, is the floor done yet?" When given the okay, they rushed the floor and began to slip and slide, twist and jerk, and carry on every which way to get every spot of the linoleum buffed. We had a ball twisting and shouting and bumping into each other, saying, *Mi scusi* ("Excuse me"). Over time we added music; the older girls insisted on teaching the younger boys how to dance. Occasionally, someone would get inspired and try to organize next year's cast of floating fairies for the *Nutcracker*. The most memorable was simply pretending to be human bumper cars.

Setting up the bar in the kitchen was next. The process began when we brought out our mother's good, star-cut glasses, which were used only on special occasions such as the New Year's Eve party. We dared not to break one, fearing some ancestral curse. The contents were gingerly taken out of their boxes and arranged to make the bar look presidential.

One of the most menial jobs, but one we considered fun, was taking the guests' coats when they arrived the night of the party. We greeted them at the front door, which had a handsome coatroom area with marble floor and leaded glass windows. After a quick greeting, we whisked the coats up to our parent's bed. By the time the party got rolling, the coats were a few layers deep. This made finding the right coats a challenge when the guests left. After a while, we resorted to finding coats according to the owner's perfume or cologne—"Get [so and so's] coat; you know, the one that smells like an old granny."

The middle children bragged about how much they received in tips when they returned the coats; the younger ones would already be in bed and unfortunately not get a cut. It was never clear if the good family and friends gave a coat tip, since we dared not to discuss it in front of our parents. This gave our mother one more action of ours to be "mortified" over.

Around 10:00 p.m., the youngest children were summarily dismissed to bed. They went begrudgingly, but knew this was not a life sentence. They would sneak down to the mid-level landing of the front steps that gave a view of the foyer, which was a high-traffic area. They took delight in spotting who was who and giggled trying to guess what each was drinking. Once in a while, someone spotted them and waved hello. They moved back when it was an older sibling, as they would expose them for encroachment—just for fun. A daring move was descending a few steps in order to sneak a gander at the dining room, which housed much of the food. The back steps were tempting as a lookout, but proved too risky. While it would give a close-up of who was at the bar, it was too deep into the off-limits territory, and if one of the other kids closed the back door, they would be trapped and caught for sure.

The next and more liberating job was serving the food and drinks. There was never a dry guest in the house as half-dozen kids attended to the guests constantly inquiring, "Hey, do you need another drink?" We always felt that getting the drinks was kind of neat, but required staying close to our parents for fear of being sent back upstairs with the younger kids. Another concern was when the older siblings took liberties with the younger children by bossing them around. As our mother noted, "Whenever I give a job to one of the kids, she goes out and gets an assistant." So true.

There was always good cheer around the bar, and the bartender usually liked to talk about the guest to whom we were serving a drink. "Now you tell your Uncle Johnny that he has to stop smoking that cigar because it makes your mother sick; she has enough children to reprimand and does not want to add her little brother to the list." One year an older sister's boyfriend, who posed as someone much older, became the self-proclaimed bartender. Turned out he was under age. After that incident, every bartender had to be of family blood, and our father checked the person's ID.

There was a room for everyone's pleasure on New Year's, oddly similar to the room set up in the board game, Clue®. Quiet discussion or even a chess game took place in our father's library (the study). The living room was packed with older couples getting reacquainted with those they had not seen for a long time. The kitchen had all kinds of activity, including the bar and first samplings of any food making rounds to the table or being served to the guests. The downstairs was filled with pool sharks and teenage cousins and friends strategizing whom they would want to be near when the New Year rang in. The dining room was filled with substantive food and the best fruits, nuts, desserts, and candies that guests brought.

As midnight approached, we went into the pantry and got the pots and pans to clang on the front porch while we screamed, "Happy New Year." And something unusual happened; our mother stepped out of character. She asked to have a chair placed in the middle of the room and for someone to hand her a dollar bill. She would raise the dollar above her head at the stroke of midnight. Upon seeing such a sight, someone ran to get our father from the study. She then asked for her Mummers outfit, as she would do a Mummers strut as good luck in the coming year.

Here was a woman who could have easily asked for $100 to account for the luck needed to move sixteen children through to another year. As her performance began, the radio went on and everyone got ready to cheer.

Our parents were never melancholy on New Year's. Regardless of the sad events during the year—sons in the military, deaths of loved ones—they smiled and looked forward to another year.

As the years went by and the family grew, more and more people came to our New Year's party. It was tradition. Looking back over the years with all of those functions and events—from birthday celebrations, to backyard picnics, to haunted houses, to high holy days—New Year's was a time of joy for the blessings of the past year and the hope of a good year ahead. Yet while no one went out on New Year's Eve, we all knew our family party was better than being in Times Square.

## CHAPTER 5
# Vacations at the Shore
ℭ℞

**THE JERSEY SHORE**

DECIDING ON WHERE TO GO for the family vacation is an important criterion for whether a marriage will work. There are the mountains people, camping people, New England shore people, the Carolinas people, etc. But true Philadelphians vacation at the shore—the New Jersey shore that is. Not the seashore, not the beach house, not the oceanfront—the shore. Then there was the decision of which shore—northern or southern Jersey—the family wanted to go to. Our family tried both, but we ended up going north, i.e., anything above Long Beach Island, New Jersey.

**YOU ONLY NEED ONE.**

Buying a house can be taxing, and our parents believed "you just need one." Renting a house at the Jersey shore for a few weeks with sixteen children was equally taxing, especially given that our parents were split on where to rent—north or south. As children, we really did not care; we just wanted to be at the shore, any shore.

Soon after New Year's, our parents traveled to New Jersey to find a place to rent. Upon their return, we were eager to learn which shore we would vacation that summer: Avalon? Sea Isle City? Would it be situated on the ocean? The bay? And would we be near friends from school? Our mother said that real estate agents believed she was fronting for an underage clan, who wanted an extended senior week. Who needed that many rooms and that many beds?

One year our father informed us that we were staying at one of the religious sisters' retreat houses. "It is perfect," he said. "The chapel is just down the hall." We looked at him and thought, "What? Isn't this supposed to be our vacation?" When he told us we each would have our own room, we cried, "When do we go?"

While the sisters' residence could accommodate our family, the housing logistics involved more than the number of rooms. We had to consider the appropriate number of beds, the male/female splits, and the age differences, which made the process very interesting. A few years, in fact, there were not enough beds, so we simply loaded a few extra beds (all pieces) into a truck and transported them to the shore. On one occasion, we rented a house from our mother's sister, which did not go over well with our eleven first cousins who had their summer vacation at the shore cut short.

The older kids teased that we moved to various shores because the lifeguards got tired of whistling at us for breaking the beach rules. Turns out, we were victims of convenience. They figured that one of the unruly kids on the beach was most likely someone from our group.

But no matter what the reason, we did not care which shore was chosen. Moving along the Jersey coastline was neat because there was always an interesting story to tell about each particular shore location—which had the highest dune, the biggest waves, the nicest sand, or the fastest rides. That was the beauty of the Jersey shore; each little town or borough had its own unique character.

## THE VACATION LOAD OUT

We always knew when vacation was approaching. Our older brothers were instructed to go to the third-floor storage room, bring down the big white storage boxes, and then distribute one to each sibling.

The boxes had a picture of a Quaker on them and some of us assumed these were the same boxes that held bulk amounts of oatmeal, which we ate in huge quantities during the winter months. The older ones said the boxes were not from a cereal company but a moving company. Being from Philly, we then inquired why Benjamin Franklin, who was a Quaker and famous Philadelphian, did not have his picture on the storage box. Annoyed by the litany of questions, the older siblings sent one of the younger kids downstairs to ask our mother why we are not using the Catholic boxes to move to the shore. We never did get a straight answer about that one.

Another indicator of vacation approaching was top-to-bottom housecleaning involving more than just the first floor cleaning done for the holidays. Trying to get out of the chore, we reasoned to our mother that in a few weeks the house would get dusty, so why not just clean it once upon our return? As with Christmas, the stakes were high, and the threat was always, "If you don't do [such and such a thing], you can spend the vacation in the hot, hot city with [so and so relative]." Her threat played well even when we were at the shore, because invariably our father had to go back to the hospital to check on patients, so our mother remarked, "And if you don't behave, you will accompany your father back to the hot, hot city while he is seeing his patients." Horrors!

The kitchen overflowed with boxes. Every cabinet was opened as our mother spewed order after order as one of us scribbled notes on a piece of paper, a bag or the boxes while someone was looking for tape or scissors. Confused by the task that we were clearing out all our household food supply, we asked if there were supermarkets at the shore. Our mother noted that it was best to bring as many dry goods as possible—whatever that meant.

The ride to the shore was about two hours, so the tradition was to go early in the morning to the corner store to buy provisions for the long drive. This usually consisted of buying a can of soda, which was wrapped in aluminum foil, gum, Sugar Daddy® taffy, and anything else that would last the journey. Chocolate was forbidden, since our mother did not believe in air conditioning (we were told we would gain graces for bearing the heat). The older kids told us that they don't sell chocolate at the shore because it melts easily, which seemed like more of a reason to bring some. Some of us got the idea to dig out old Easter candy, which we had squirreled away. In the end, we realized they were right; chocolate never fared well on a ride to the shore. We soon understood why the Jersey shore sold so much salt-water taffy.

It was a well-known fact to stay clear of the kitchen otherwise you were put to work. One job was to "go see what your father is doing; he may need help." He was usually found in the study surveying what books to bring on vacation. Not only did he invest time in his own books, but each year he discovered the latest educational fad and packed skill-building books for us.

While we thought we were off the hook from school work, our father had other plans. He required that we read and build our academic skills during summer vacation. This even annoyed our mother. She was working hard to pack a house for the shore, while our father was worried about what books to bring. Plus, the books were heavy, and she reminded him to the square inch how much room was available in the two to three cars plus the truck after the family was loaded in—not much.

Equipped with our one storage box, we packed our personal necessities. The art of packing involved not only deciding which clothes to bring but to take advantage of the mayhem by appropriating another sibling's clothes.

Our older brothers would start at the top floor and pass by each room (just once) to pick up our clothes boxes to load onto the truck. They warned us that if we did not have our box ready and outside our room, we were stuck going to the shore with just the clothes on our backs. This made us anxious, so we stayed up all night fearful that we would oversleep and not have a box ready for the shore.

**THE CARAVAN TO THE SHORE**

We looked forward to the arrival of our mother's brother who rented and drove the big truck to the shore filled with our provisions. The minute he stepped into our house, he caused panic by yelling upstairs to our mother, "Mary, I have a very tight schedule today, so let's get things moving." (He had nine children of his own.) He was one who could get our mother flustered.

The truck's cab could only fit three people, including the driver. We came of age when we got to ride in the truck. Driving with Uncle John meant you were the first to leave and first to arrive. More important, we were told that those in the truck were treated to ice cream along the way. Boy, it was disappointing when we found out he did not stop for ice cream. "Is that what the other kids told you?" he asked laughingly.

We vied to ride in the other cars. Not many wanted to accompany our father, because he drove too slowly and listened to talk radio. Even more disconcerting was the time he spent quizzing us on the finer points of medicine and theology, as well as "How is your Latin?" or "What are you learning in school nowadays?" Similar to the dinnertime questions, these questions had no apparent answers, just thought provoking. Any strategy to divert the questioning seemed to backfire. An older kid would whisper a wrong answer in one of the younger kid's ear, thus causing our father to expand not only on the right answer, but why the silly answer could not possibly be right. So much for the diversion strategy.

We invested time on who would ask our father to stop for ice cream promising each other we would not tell the others. This promoted a discussion about the virtues of honesty and the principles of distributed justice, just about the time we drove by the ice cream stand.

It was not uncommon for our father to be called "back to the hot city" to see a patient. Our mother requested that one of the older boys accompany him home. They did a quick "rock, paper, scissors" to see who would go, knowing they would be subjected to more talk radio and quizzing. Often on the ride back he said, "Let's say the rosary; it will pass the time." This type of recitation naturally put someone to sleep. If our father seemed sleepy, we suggested that he place the rosary recital in abeyance; it is not safe. He agreed and would pull over to the side of the road to complete the recitation.

Riding with our mother meant there was enough food to last cross-country. This was comforting to know if we, in fact, were stranded in the Jersey Pine Barrens, home of the "Jersey Devil." The older kids told us that no amount of food would satisfy the Jersey Devil, since he only ate little kids. If we left later when there was an overcast sky, we did not mind saying a rosary to get us safely through the Pine Barrens before dark. Mentioning a stop at the ice cream stand was out of the question.

When our mother left for the shore, she stopped for nobody and nothing. It was Jersey shore or bust for her. We spent many trips "holding it in," and if we complained about needing to go to the bathroom, she reminded us that drinking a can of soda on the ride down to the shore was not a good idea.

In later years there would be one more car piloted by an edgy teen driver whose main goal was to beat the oldest sibling's record for arrival at the shore. While it was exciting to ride in this car, there were times when we feared for our lives as the driver whisked around the many infamous New Jersey roadway circles. Others were back-seat drivers, who argued that, "Mother does not go this way," and that we were going to end up in New York, and even though Coney Island looked cool on TV, it was uncharted waters for us. We were comforted that we were on the right track when someone would roll the window down, and say he could smell the salt air, and as long as we were going east and south, we would eventually reach the Atlantic Ocean. Ironically, this car was the last one to arrive at the shore house, blaming the delay on "taking a wrong turn coming onto the island." Actually, they arrived in plenty of time but proceeded straight to the boardwalk to see the new rides. They also knew that arriving last meant fewer boxes for them to unload from the truck. "There are plenty of others to unload the truck," they reasoned.

## SAND IN THE BED, DAMPNESS IN THE AIR, AND THE SOUND OF THE OCEAN WAVES HITTING THE SURF

Even though it had been a full year since we had seen the ocean, our mother announced, "Nobody goes up to the ocean until all the work is done around here." Not only did we unpack, but we had to clean the rental home. We all had our own ideas on how to form an assembly line to unload the truck. It only took one kid leaning the wrong way for the system to fail.

Our Uncle John reminded us that he only drives the truck. "There are plenty of able-bodied kids here to unload this thing." Even though he was not short on direction on how we should unload the truck, he wanted it done in a hurry. "I have to get the truck back to the rental shop, and if I am late and have to pay extra, I am asking your father to take it out of your allowances."

One trick we devised for seeing the ocean was when our uncle was leaving. A couple of kids explained to our mother that we were accompanying him to the gas station before he left. "Good idea," she concurred. This bought us our first look at the ocean since the previous year, for which we were forever grateful to him.

There was added excitement on the first night as we were guaranteed a new roommate. Our mother allowed us to shuffle the deck. It was neat to find out how the other siblings lived in their rooms. We came up with some interesting combinations. One house actually had numbers on the door, so when we arrived, a list was put up with names beside each bedroom accompanied by a number. Each night we went to sleep with sand in the bed, dampness in the air, and the non-reproducible sound of the ocean waves hitting the surf. It was summertime at the shore!

## THE NUANCES OF A SUMMER RENTAL

Even the most mundane tasks were a time of discovery and adventure for us in our summer rental home. By the first full day, our mother began operating the house as if she had lived there her entire life. No rental property developer had us in mind, so we adjusted. But some rentals had remarkable features. One had only one bathroom resulting in several accidents that summer. If that wasn't bad enough, it had two entrances, one from the second-floor corridor, and the other from a back bedroom. That bedroom also had a door that led to a second set of back steps. This provided an opportunity for a prankster to go into the bathroom and then go down the back steps to see how long it took for the bathroom line to back up with people screaming for the occupier to "Hurry up; I am going to burst."

One house had no basement nor outside shower, so our mother bathed the younger kids in the utility sinks. Another house had cacti as a lawn covering, which seemed like an odd lawn covering. Our mother and the older siblings spent hours clipping cactus splinters out of our feet. (To this day, some of us are scarred and can never take our shoes off, even at the shore.)

Our grandmother, the seamstress, had a unique way of removing splinters. She took a long, thick sewing needle and dug into the skin. The procedure was quick but painful. She first stuck the needle in her thumb and said, "See, this does not hurt." Needles to say, she had tough skin from years of pushing needles with her thumbs.

One year we rented a house that was too close to the ground with no basement. As a result, crickets roamed the place seeking shelter in our shoes. To this day, some of us check our sneakers before putting them on just in case a cricket found our shoes to be a comfortable spot.

Several houses had two kitchens, but the rental with the kitchen on the second floor made a convenient excuse for us on why we were not helping with chores (e.g., "Oh I went to the kitchen to help and nothing was happening."). Not all the houses had washers or dryers, so we spent plenty of time in the laundromat. One consolation to going to the laundromat was that we were allowed to read comic books and chew gum there. There were few houses with any amenities. It could be hotter than July and our mother would still say, "If you keep still, you will not be hot."

**LET'S GO TO THE BEACH.**

Storming the beach was a one-shot deal. There was no going early, coming back for lunch at noon, and then returning. Now that would have been nice, but required too much work. So our mother, the master of timing meals, served breakfast as late as possible. As a result, we were not hungry for lunch thus avoiding a return trip to the beach house.

Getting maximum time at the beach meant staying until 4:00 p.m., so by the end of the day, we were both famished and tired. This provided a tempered persona among all. It began properly with hanging our bathing suits and towels on the back yard clothesline. No beach paraphernalia was permitted anywhere other than this designated spot. God forbid there would be a towel on the porch railing hanging to dry, or a swimsuit left hanging in the shower room. Our mother was clear explaining to us what the shore house was not, e.g., frat house, hotel, etc.

**THE SUMMER PROJECT**

Our father was not one for the beach. Each summer he chose a major project, which he worked on when not reading about medicine or theology. Note that he was not schooled in the arts but somehow got inspired during the summer.

One summer, our father made a chess board out of black and white tiles and various shells to represent all the pieces. Our favorite was the horse, made from a sea horse, of course. We drove about thirty-minutes up the coast to the shell shop. It took a number of trips, some trial and error, but it was a fabulous summer project that remains in the family today.

Another summer, our father decided he wanted to learn how to play the ukulele. We learned all kinds of American folk songs that summer. And in good form, our father put some local color into the lyrics. This was one of our favorites:

*Oh, you can't get to heaven*
*(Oh, you can't get to heaven)*

*On the LBJ*

*(On the LBJ,)*

*'Cause the LBJ*

*('Cause the LBJ)*

*Don't go that way.*

*(Don't go that way.)*

*Oh you can't get to heaven on the LBJ,*

*'Cause the LBJ don't go that way.*

*I ain't gonna grieve my Lord no more.*

## SKILL BUILDING IN THE SUMMERTIME

While the major project changed for our father each summer, the skill-building kits remained standard fare for us. Our mother secretly sided with us that summer was a time for sun, sand, and surf. But our father continued to purchase mega learning kits, such as Hooked on Phonics®, speed reading, Math Made Easy®, How to Build a Better Vocabulary®, and other "fun" ways to learn.

Our father reasoned "we have more time on your hands to read" during the summer. Brief classic novels, such as *Lord of the Flies* or *Animal Farm*, were not acceptable reading during the summer months. We had to step it up with something substantive such as *Great Expectations, The Grapes of Wrath,* or *Main Street.* If we complained, our father threatened us with *War and Peace* or *The Fall of the Roman Empire.*

Shore towns had mobile libraries. One year, our father managed to get the mobile library driver to park in front of the house. To him this was convenient; to us it was geeky. "But what if by accident we miss the return date and we are back in the city?" Our father already accounted for that. He had the coordinates of the stationary library and figured the director would not think that a physician would stiff them of children and teenage books.

Our father did redeem himself. If he had to return to the city to see patients, he came back with a box of fun things to do, such as paint by numbers, puzzles, model cars and airplanes, and plaster Disney® characters to paint.

Given our father was risk averse, we learned everything we needed to know to be safe around the bay and sea. First and foremost, we took swim lessons. No temped, calm YMCA or public swimming pool for this. It was in the Barnegat Bay at 8:00 a.m. where the water was freezing and the wind was cutting. The instructors never smiled and as we got older, we understood why. The biggest motivator for learning how to swim was the bay was murky and filled with icky, itchy seaweed plus the threat of a Jersey Blue Claw Crab pinching our feet. Eventually, we learned to swim as far out as we could until the lifeguards whistled us in.

Boating was another required safety skill. First was learning how to row a boat, not only by ourselves, but with a passenger in case we were the true captain of the ship. Another trick required rowing and towing another boat. One summer, one of the boys did so much rowing that he seriously blistered his hands, which subsequently got infected and he soon developed the infamous "red line," or infection. We were familiar with the red line being children of mother who was a nurse and a father physician.

As much as our parents warned us not to walk around in bare feet, we had our share of cuts from broken bottles, nails, sharp wood and other debris along the bay or under the boardwalk. We kept our parents skilled at giving a tetanus shot. If it was our father giving the shot, we asked him, "Shouldn't Mother be doing this?" Needless to say, he was not pleased with us questioning his clinical skills.

The next lesson was sailing. Everyone had to learn the three levels of vessel navigation—small, medium and large. We were dry-docked until we took the boating seamanship course, advanced boating seamanship, and a sundry of American Red Cross water safety courses. The process for learning how to drive a car was far easier.

The nautical skill building did pay off. By the time we completed our lessons, we could navigate anything from a small dinghy sailboat to a

20-foot sail catamaran. We could row across the Barnegat Bay and back (close to a three-mile trip), and could read a nautical map, nautical waterway signs and buoys, and nautical flags.

We enjoyed the many treats of the bay, from waterskiing, to navigating though lagoons, to tying up the boats and jumping off bridges to swim, to all kinds of fishing and late-night crabbing.

One afternoon, a few of the younger boys took their command of the bay seriously and paddled surfboards to the other side of the bay and back, about one and three quarters of a mile each way. The trip involved crossing three major channels. Needles to say, our mother was concerned. A neighbor heard the commotion and offered to take her boat to the boys and bring them back safely. Upon reaching them, she convinced the two younger ones to get in the boat but the oldest one held out to claim bragging rights. (Ostensibly, several nephews and nieces have claimed to make the trip, but there is scant evidence.)

While we loved the ocean, the bay was ours. Eventually, we settled on the bay in Seaside Park, New Jersey, and became known as "the Bay People." On the bay, the sunrise over the ocean was glorious and the sunset mystifying. And even though it was a lot of work for our parents to take us to the shore, our mother said seeing the sunset in the bay is one of life's greatest pleasures.

## THAT RAINY DAY FEELING...

What do you do at the shore with a large family on a rainy or overcast day? Any family on vacation dreads a rainy day, especially without a decent television. Back in those days, there was really "nothing good on." Watching sports in the northern shore region was a problem since all the stations carried the New York baseball teams, not the Phillies. Solution? Put on a play.

Putting on a play incorporated everyone's talents. There were the prima donna actors and actresses, the writers, the directors, the stage crew, and a captive audience. The event culminated in one of our greatest shore treats—boardwalk pizza!

Our grandmothers provided another solution to our rainy day doldrums. They loved to play games. One taught us how to play Canasta, which she always had to win. Apparently in "the old country" (Italy), cheating was part of the game. When she played our other grandmother, it was not a pretty site; she was an upstanding Christian woman and cheating had no business in her card games.

Our one grandmother organized major Bingo games at her sister's vacation home at the same shore. We would all cram into a small house just a little bit bigger than a bungalow and play Bingo for hours hoping to win candy prizes. She was fair and played no favorites; we only received the candy prize commensurate with our wins. No wins, no candy, no matter your age.

Other times we went to the movies. One year was the first run of the movie, *Flipper*. When we arrived at the theatre, we discovered it was a double feature. We had to sit through *How to Stuff a Wild Bikini*, starring a Philly Fab, Frankie Avalon, and his girl, Annette Funicello. One brother held his head down ostensibly due to the racy nature of the beach party movie. While one brother assured him that our parents would never find out he was watching a racy movie, he did not change his position. To everyone's surprise, he complained of having extreme pain in his stomach, which one brother attributed to eating a milk caramel sucker. He said that he hadn't touched his candy because his side hurt.

Soon the pain got worse, and he started to cry not just from the pain, but at the thought that he had ruined the others from seeing *Flipper*. All ten kids had to leave the theater. The pain was so bad he could hardly walk so one of our brothers carried him home for several blocks on his shoulders. When they arrived, three physicians—our father, an uncle and a friend who was also a physician—examined him. They quickly diagnosed him as having an inflamed appendix that required having an appendectomy. Shocked, our mother argued, "That cannot be it. How could he have appendicitis? He is only six years old?" The three physicians looked at each other puzzled and did not say a word. Our mother wrapped him in a blanket to make the drive back to Philadelphia with our father.

Our brother had little memory of what transpired next. All he recalled was waking up in a pediatric ward. None of the child patients believed that he had so many siblings when he told them about us. Even when a nurse showed up with a dozen or so handmade get well cards, they were still doubtful. An older kid said they were from classmates, but our brother asked him how could that be so, since school had not started yet.

## FAMILY NIGHT AT THE SHORE

As we got older, our father instituted family night at least once during each of the few weeks we were at the shore. Horrors! Who wants to stay in during vacation? We wanted to hang out on the beach, walk under the boardwalk, or go on the amusement rides. But the rule was "nobody out." Since he did not say "nobody in," we invited our friends over. We actually had a neat time making up various games to play. Given that there were many prepubescent children and teenagers in the group, there was enough energy to entertain each other. At the end of the night, we were rewarded with boardwalk pizza.

## HOME ALONE

Of course the real big night at the shore was going to the boardwalk for the amusement rides. It was the topic of the week. It seemed like the time would never come.

Venturing to the boardwalk with a large family was not a feat that our mother did by herself. She recruited her youngest sibling and other adults, who were assigned a group of children to mind. It was like going on a field trip.

Keeping count of children was made with every move. There was never a problem with the count. The problem was nobody double-checked just how many did we consider taking. On one occasion, a four-year-old brother was truly left home alone. Tired after a long day at the beach, he slipped upstairs for a nap. When our mother went back to retrieve him, he was sound asleep. When she woke him, he asked if it was time to go to the boardwalk. Our mother said, "Sure!"

## READY-MADE TEAMS

A big advantage of large extended families is there are always enough kids to play a game—any game. No need to recruit the neighbors; there were instant teams anytime we wanted to play something. Whether low-key games such as "Mother May I," "Guess which hand [the penny is in]," "Ducks Have Feathers," "Red Light; Green Light" or fast-moving games such as run the bases, dodge ball, baby-in-the-air, jail break, or buck-buck, we took over any playground simply by showing up.

Often, other kids joined our group or involved us in what they were doing. Being bullied was never a problem, as any scream for help created an instant posse. Herd mentality had a lot of advantages.

It was important to have off-the-shelf games when the group could not move around, such as the two-hour car drive to the shore. These included the obligatory name a word on a sign with a letter starting with A through the alphabet to Z, or memorizing games with a litany of things such as "My mother went to the store and bought Apples—A," or " I spy a color with my naked eye that is ____," or "I am thinking of a famous person, place, or thing with the initials ____." These were our parents' favorites, as they kept the volume down and caused little arguing.

While vacation is a time for respite and an escape from everyday life, it seemed that events during the summer were more acute, finding a special place in our memories. The music was more exciting during the summer, and the movies seemed edgier. We witnessed some of the most significant historical events of the time while at the seashore, such as the Civil Rights riots, the landing on the moon, Woodstock, the Vietnam War, and the resignation of President Nixon. Our father often said that "a retreat is not a flight from life, but a journey into its meaning."

## THE SIMPLE THINGS OF SUMMER

Sometimes it was just fun doing something simple. In the 1960s when gas was cheap, we piled into our station wagon and another car and went joyriding. There are so many things to see for free at the Jersey shore, like driving to chartered fishing boats sites to watch workers unload the catch of the day. We drove to one of the inlets and watched the boats moving in and out while negotiating the choppy water with little room for error. We visited the Barnegat Bay Lighthouse and rolled down the highest dunes in New Jersey. We sifted for diamonds in Cape May and looked for sunken ships. We climbed Lucy the Elephant in Margate and visited Island Beach State Park or Pelican Island, both of which seemed peculiarly deserted. Sometimes we simply rode along a bay front or the ocean and looked at the neat houses. Our mother usually said something such as, "How would you like to have to clean all of those windows?" And while we were not invited to too many places as a family, our parents were creative in making a simple car trip be something interesting to do.

Kids can never have enough excitement in a day, especially on vacation. Many nights, we asked our mother to tell us a scary story. There were some stories that no matter how often they were told, they were still scary. One such story was *The Golden Leg*. It tells the tale of an old lady, who has a golden leg and dies. The surviving sister takes the leg off before burial. Then one stormy night, the sister returns to haunt the other sister and reclaim the golden leg.

Other stories included the *Monkey's Paw* and *The Blue Baby* when each year on August 8 (about the time of our vacation) a baby would haunt any room that was blue because of a tragic crib death from a lightning strike. No one slept in a blue bedroom every August 8. Our oldest brother was a great, scary storyteller and occasionally took over for our mother. Of course, all of this was morbid and was cause for bed hopping by the little ones.

Our mother would also sing to us. Our favorite was the late 19th century song by Gussie Davis, *In the Baggage Coach Ahead*.

Big families did not go to Disneyworld, take a European tour, vacation on an exotic tropical island, or hobnob with the rich and famous on the Cape. Our vacations were unpretentious, and we were thankful.

We went to sleep the last night of vacation with sand in the bed, dampness in the air, and the sound of ocean waves hitting the surf.

# Our home, *Pro Deo et Patria*
## ("For God and Country")

Pen and Ink by John Maxwell

## CHAPTER 6
# This is not a democracy.
ભ

**WHATEVER YOUR MOTHER SAYS GOES.**

OUR FATHER WAS VERY CLEAR about the political system in which we would operate. On numerous occasions and at teachable moments, he said, "This is not a democracy." Our parents were the rule givers and privilege takers when some semblance of order did not exist and, most important, if we did not act in good faith nor in good form.

It may seem harsh to suggest that we lived under the rule of two dictators. Well, maybe one. And that one was our mother emboldened by our father. He made it clear that, "Whatever your mother says goes. "If she says 'jump,' you say 'how high.' If she puts sawdust on your plate, you will eat the sawdust without complaint." In fact, the pope, whom one would think is a higher-order sovereign, was easily trumped by my mother's wishes.

This directive about "Who rules?" usually came at very tense times when we were all out of control, and our father was beside himself. He would exclaim, "I don't care if the pope comes into the house and tells you to [insert command here], what your mother says goes." Directives worked best by such fiat.

Such hyperbole was interesting coming from a man who usually was quite risk averse. For example, the jumping command did not exist with any sibling. When in trouble a pat answer was to say an older brother or sister "told me to do [the act]." He would say: "If [older sibling] told you to jump off a bridge, would you jump off of a bridge? Of course not!"

## "I OWN EVERYTHING IN THIS HOUSE."

We learned early that we really owned nothing (as much as we thought we lived in a commune), not even the things closest to our person, literally. For example, with nine girls each close in age, it was common for one sister to "borrow" another sister's clothes or the boys' clothes when style permitted. This caused common rants of "Who took my bell-bottom jeans?" "Where is my favorite shirt?" "Mother, Susanne took my sweater again, and she did not even wash it. She needs to give it back to me washed." "Who took my gym shorts?" The rants went on and on until my father announced, "Enough! Nobody took anything from anyone. I own everything in this house." The announcement was so peculiar to us, we had to stop and think about it. Could this mean we were indentured? More important, if he was willing to make claim on our personal wardrobes, what was next? This tempered the rants at least until the next weekend when we did not have to wear school uniforms, and the family wardrobe was up for grabs.

## LAUNDRY: DIVIDE AND CONQUER

People wondered how our family handled laundering clothes. As with so many temporal matters, our mother created a system and recruited support. To begin there were two—and only two—dirty clothes drop-off locations. Clothesbaskets were in the second and third floor hallways, the only acceptable locations for laundry. If our mother was on the first floor and heard footsteps in the second floor hallway, she periodically called up and said, "Whoever is walking up there, please bring down that basket of clothes to the basement, so I can get them washed." If she was on the second floor, she used the same system, just called up to one of us to bring them to the basement. The nuance to the third floor was the boys (the locations of the boys' three bedrooms) could take a lazy way out and dump the clothes from the third floor into the second floor basket, avoiding going down an extra flight to the basement. The trick, of course, was not to be seen by our mother or sisters on the second floor, and with nine girls roaming that area, this was not easy to pull off.

The washer machine and dryer were oversized but not industrial. The laundry room had many pipes running just below the ceiling, which doubled as dry cleaner racks. Once a mass of clothes was assembled in the basement, she sorted them by color and water temperature. By devising a system, she only had to do the initial load; the children were co-opted to complete the assembly line of clothes washing.

My mother's system was simple. She knew when a load of wash would complete its cycle at which time she said to whoever was in earshot, "Can you open the basement door and hear if the washer is still running?" If one of the boys was present, he would reply, "No," in which case our mother simply said, "Then would you please go down there and switch the load of clothes to the dryer." If a girl was asked, she understood that the question was more than rhetorical and, rather than hear the second directive, she went downstairs and tended to the next step in the washing process. Getting the clothes back upstairs was another clever skill. She knew once she got us to the basement, as if she had forgotten, she asked us to bring up any clothes that were finished.

The folding and ironing of clothes took place on the kitchen table. Fewer commands were necessary for this step, since it was mandatory to confiscate our washed clothes before anyone else could. It was a matter of preserving our wardrobe. As we sorted through the basket, our mother simply asked us to fold the rest of the clothes for the others.

The process was never-ending. The folded items were placed in their appropriate piles. Several piles formed during the day and by the time we returned home from school or play on the weekends, we grabbed our piles and took them to our rooms. But we also saw this as an opportunity to appropriate someone else's clothes, which initiated the aforementioned ongoing complaints about who took clothes from whom. In the long run, our mother appreciated the survival game, as it bought us to do our own wash at a relatively early age. "If you want your clothes available to your person, you do your own clothes" thereby requiring less work, and steps, for her.

### LANGUAGES WERE LEARNED FOR LAW AND ORDER.

Our father was very creative with directives. For emphasis he used different languages other than English. Naturally Italian was used and German from his military service during World War II. Latin was spoken when he wanted us to think. Certainly, Latin did the trick. We assumed it was necessary to take two languages in high school (Latin and another) not so much to be a global citizen, but to acquiesce to law and order in the home.

Corralling the children is usually a challenge for any parent. To move our group, the directive *Andiamo* worked ("Let's go" in Italian). There were several German expressions but popular expressions were *Schweigen sie* ("Silence, you!") and the directive to sit down, *Hinsetzen*. When things got really bad, these two expressions were used together: *Hinsetzen und Schweigen sie*. And to move the group it was *Marschieren schnell*.

Hardly a day went by without some exposure to Latin other than through Latin prayers. Fortunately, there was a number of calm and peace-loving expressions. The phrase "Pax et bonum" was inscribed ubiquitously around the home. Once a sibling thought he would impress his sixth grade teacher by forgoing the obligatory A.M.D.G. at the top of the page of his essay (*Ad maiorem Dei gloriam*, "For the greater glory of God") and substituting it with *Pax et bonum*. This did not go over well with the good sister and a note came home describing the recalcitrant child's act. Our father did not overreact; he was enamored that his son used Latin. We saw this as a victory for us. However, the problem came when our father quizzed him with other expressions, which were thrown into the mix for easy translation. Our brother was stumped and stumped again.

When an older sister attending an all-Catholic girls school thought she would impress the family by using a literary reference—just to break the tension—she announced, "It's the scene in James Joyce's *A Portrait of the Artist as a Young Man.*" (An early scene in this novel is of a group of boarding school boys failing their Latin recitation.) Our father turned to our sister, who was quite proud, and asked, "How would you like to translate the *Twelve Labors of Hercules* from the Latin?"

The Latin phrases worked best during arguments. This was when our father became most animated. When asked why something happened in which we obfuscated by changing the temporal nature of things, he exclaimed, *Post hoc ergo propter hoc.* This is a time-honored mistake to claim that things happened simply because one followed the other.

Our *post-hoc-ergo-propter-hoc* arguments were most frequently used when we weren't feeling well. Our father, who was not one for simplicity, evaluated our condition by using a medical model. Invariably we forgot that he only wanted us to give symptoms not a diagnosis. Of course, we presented our best-guess diagnosis, such as "I know I have mono." This put him in a tailspin. "I only want symptoms, please. And what medical school did you graduate from?" Anyone below a fifth grade education, especially a boy, does not understand this type of rhetorical question. One brother figured he would give this one a try and replied, St. Charles, which was the city's Catholic seminary. Our father was speechless.

*Nota bene* ("Note well") was used liberally. When "your hand was caught in the cookie jar," you quickly got *Res ipsa loquitur* ("The thing speaks for itself"). This certainly did not seem like good due process. However, in an odd way they took on the dictatorship role with no helpers. They were not interested in any tattletale stories, as hard as we tried.

Our parents devised a litmus test of three questions for us to use when reporting on the questionable actions of a sibling. Question 1: "Is it true?" This was easy because we observed the infraction and believed in *Res ipsa loquitur*. Question 2: "Is it necessary?" Of course, the rule of law and order and good faith and good form were observed, so why should one of the others get away with something? Question 3, which was the deal breaker: "Is it kind?" Truth be told, we failed to answer in the affirmative to this question. Therefore, the tattletails were kept to a minimum.

This litmus test for telling [on someone] worked both ways. This was the "W[in]," maybe the only one that went to our side. Telling on another sibling, when asked, was taboo. That is how we survived; it just made sense. But like most parents, they wanted to know who was the culprit. The prisoner's dilemma did not work on us. We did not tell, period. If pushed, we would blame someone for whom it would be very difficult to validate, such as the sibling who was in another state, away at college or deployed by the military. This exhausted our mother.

We grew up knowing that if our parents found out something bad, they would be stricken with a cardiovascular incident. For mother it was always, "If she finds out, she will have a stroke," and for father it was "If he finds out, he will have a myocardia infarction." (Later this was shortened to him having an "M.I.") Therefore, therapeutic privilege was argued when asked, "Who did [this, that or the other thing]."

There was no risk getting into trouble for something done at school, unless it was a bad report card. In our house, the cardinal rule was, "What happens at school, stays at school, and what happens at home, stays at home."

## FIVE MINUTES OF HOLY SILENCE!

It was difficult finding a quiet place in our home. Ideally, one could get peace doing homework at an assigned desk in a bedroom. However, the odds favored constantly having someone out and about making noise. When the noise level rose or there was an overwhelming cacophony of sound, our father would announce, "Ok, that is enough. We will now have five minutes of Holy Silence."

The Holy Silence directive always came with a condition—a continuous five minutes of silence not cumulative. If a single noise was uttered, the clock was reset to the five-minute mark. As children, we could never do it; the series of mishaps was too tempting with too many options for breaking the Holy Silence. Most often, the younger kids needed clarity on defining Holy Silence and how it differed from regular silence, which caused a stream of discussion. Additionally, any noise counted against us, so giggling, which frequently happened, put us back to square one. Our youngest sibling got the idea that holding her breadth would help. Upon turning red, a sibling would call for help. Naturally she was fine, but we were back to the same starting point. The real kicker was when we would get close to the five-minute mark and someone would say, "It has to be five minutes by now." Back to the start again.

**NOBODY IN AND NOBODY OUT.**

Punishments en masse were common. With so many potential suspects, our parents did not have time to vet guilt or innocence when an infraction occurred. It was easier resolved with an across-the-board punishment. A common one was, "Nobody in and nobody out."

Initially, this seemed horrible but, with so many creative minds, we devised some interesting things to do when we were confined. Usually, our confinement involved going to the lowest point (the basement) or the highest point (the storage room) in the house. Both were dark places with sundry things stored waiting for us to rummage through them.

The basement contained boxes and boxes of holiday decorations, old train sets, books, and all kinds of junk. There was also a back basement containing a separate storage area with a homegrown fallout shelter filled with jugs of water and canned food, flashlights, candles, odd-looking tools, and myriad paraphernalia. The older siblings said this is where we would go if the Martians came at which point the younger ones responded, "There are no such things as Martians." On cue, the lights went out and the screaming began.

There were several other basement rooms to retreat to, each containing some type of enclosure just waiting to swallow up a kid who needed to serve out some penance for misbehavior.

The storage room on the third floor was no safer. The spiders and their webs seemed more domestic than those in the basement. The treasures were more interesting, filled with boxes of memorabilia, chests, and makeshift closets. The older siblings would tell stories about great aunts and uncles and who owned what chest and how we inherited some of the antiquities.

Since our father never discarded a single book, there were enough literature and language books, *National Geographic* magazines, and national news weekly magazines to open up a used bookstore. The real entertainment came when thumbing through the medical journals. Our curiosity was healthy, but we paid the price. Photos of grand rounds in medical journals were not P.G. rated.

There was a cedar closet outside the storage room, but it was unclear who owned the contents. It housed dated children's outfits, which the older siblings said belonged to lost siblings. "You mean there were more of us?" We never inquired again about those clothes.

Eventually, someone got the idea to ask our mother if she needed help in the hopes that with a little servile work, we could be out on "good behavior" or at least relegated to the back yard. Cautiously, we emerged from our confines and converged into the kitchen, where our mother spent many of her waking hours.

But the kitchen was not always our safe haven for escaping punishment and chores. Our mother needed her space in the kitchen, and our bombardment was not always greeted as we hoped. There was one sweeping announcement that inevitably cleared everyone out of the kitchen. She would simply say, "The kitchen is now closed." And if there was work in progress and she needed more room, she stated, "If you stay in this kitchen you will get a job." The place usually cleared.

## WILL SHE RETURN?

Obviously, our mother spent many hours in the kitchen but not by choice. There was always constant activity and chores to be done that were centralized there. Her bedroom was public property as well. She gave up taking a quick nap there because a stream of children would, with good intentions, check up on her just to make sure she was not sick. After a half dozen door openings and children taking their turn asking, "Why are you resting. Are you sick?" she figured she could be more productive elsewhere.

Several times a year when the recalcitrance among us peaked, both in nature and the extent, our mother would make good on her threat, "If you keep this up, I am getting into that wagon and driving right away." There were times when she left, after which you could hear a pin drop in the house. We would sit on the high windowsill, look out the window, and quibble over who was to blame while hoping for her return. Most likely she told one of the older siblings that she had to do an errand but wanted to have a teachable moment. When the headlights hit the driveway and the car turned up, we jumped down from the windowsill and ran to our beds. The scare was effective for a few weeks of good behavior.

**FAMILY MEETINGS**

Our mother was never a wait-until-your-father-gets-home parent. He needed no prodding to move into his teachable moments, which took the form of "the family meeting."

Family meetings were held at the table, where our father sat at the head of the table and called the meeting to order by banging a gavel. (He used a coaster made of cork to absorb the bang. Once the head of the gavel flung off but nobody dared laugh.) The agenda was not usually clear, especially for the younger siblings.

Each meeting was prefaced with a few prayers, especially if it was a serious family issue. Our father used various medical analogies, which were usually beyond the younger siblings' comprehension, but we could always count on one of the older siblings for a good translation. While we initially groaned about attending these meetings, they really were interesting and ended with some type of treat.

The penultimate agenda item was an open forum for issues concerning the good of the order. The popular topic was the use of unwanted nicknames. Our father was not upset at this type of name-calling, since he recognized them as terms of endearment. He was genuinely interested in our creativity, but the challenge came when we used code names or letters to disguise a nickname. For example, one sister earned the nickname "Witch" because when we played the card game Old Maid®, she was always stuck with the Old Maid®. This was not a complimentary name, so we had to disguise it, at which point we simply called her "D." She explained to our father that she took umbrage with being called "D" because "D stood for dibber and dibber stood for W and W stood for Witch, so I don't want these kids calling me D." After that explanation, our father called for a moratorium on anyone calling another a single letter of the alphabet.

One part of the meeting was always clear—the jobs list. Our father would state a job then someone would raise his or her hand to claim it. Inevitably, another sibling would argue to the volunteer, "You never do that job. Mother always asks me to do it, because you never do it."

Any parent with sixteen children has to be considered a full professor of pedagogy, using any and all teaching strategies available. Our father was great with analogies and metaphors and the more graphic, the better. For example, one meeting he took a piece of paper and tore it in half saying, "See how easy it is to tear one sheet of paper?" Then he tore the paper in half again and gave it to one of the children. Then again and again until he had sixteen pieces of paper stacked. Nobody could tear the papers at that point. He then said, "So if we all stick together, it is harder to tear us apart."

The impromptu meetings were not our favorite usually due to their abrupt assemblage. Sometimes late at night, we were rousted out of bed and asked to convene in the kitchen. As we walked downstairs, we pointed fingers at those we believed caused the problems. Our mother stood off to the side and said nothing. After a few of these meetings, we realized they were in cahoots. She was the *éminence grise* on family affairs.

Our father, suited in his smoking jacket, paced back and forth. Trying to avoid eye contact with him, we dipped our heads, just in case we were the culprits. He said, "There is a cancer growing in this family, and I am going to find it and cut it out." Unaware of the nature and the extent of the "cancer," we began the litany of transgressions among the group, one by one and in painful detail. We hoped for mercy and forgiveness en masse. But it usually closed with "nobody in and nobody out, until I see that you all get the message." We were then asked to kiss our mother and return to bed.

## GETTING YOUR JUST REWARD.

The topic of our allowances was usually brought to question during family meetings. The allowances, which were housed in a small, white pill envelope, were distributed on Fridays. One of our father's office staff members placed change, or bills if you were an older sibling, in the pill envelopes. The rate never increased for years.

Once one of the younger kids suggested forming a union to determine the allowance allocations. Much to their disappointment, a union would not work, since age dictated the amount allotted to each small, white envelope.

While our father had a system, the white pill envelopes did not always come each week, but the roles of quarters, dimes, nickels, and pennies did. He stored them in a box in the trunk of his car. Over time, these rolls of cold cash grew. One spring while cleaning his car, we discovered the treasure trove. Thereafter, he had no problem getting anyone to clean his car, since we knew we would find an errant cash stash. On the other hand, we never volunteered to clean our mother's car for fear of discovering some forgotten something by a kid that looked to be a science experiment. We also knew there was never any errant cash in her car.

One time we discovered a box of rolls of coins. We knew we hit the jackpot. A clandestine, sibling family meeting was called to discuss what to do with the spoils. One of the older children convinced us that if we gave the box to our mother, we would get a reward, maybe even more than the worth of the rolls of coins. That night when all was quiet, our mother asked us to bring the box to the dining room. When our father came home, our mother asked him, "I found something of yours. Can I keep it?" Our father responded, "Natch," which was short for naturally. "What is mine is yours." We reacted in cheers and danced in the kitchen thinking we had struck gold. We don't know what happened to that box of coins; we did not see one thin dime.

Our parents were not frivolous with money; we got what was needed especially as it related to school. When an older brother asked for fifty cents (probably to buy a pack of cigarettes), our father took out a penny, placed it on the table, and said, "Don't spend it all in one place."

Our mother was the master of coin dispensing. During our high school years, she allocated money for bus and train fare, or to purchase lunch. She would place sets of coins lying on the counter like she was setting out the clothes for the day. Amazingly, she almost never forgot and if she did we would not mention it; instead we bummed money off someone else. Nobody would take more than what was allotted; it was a rule of the commune and, again, just made a lot of sense because with so many possibilities for transgressions the paybacks would not be pleasant. When it came to money, we towed the party line.

## TEENAGERS AND TRANSGRESSIONS

The neat thing about having several siblings is there is always someone who has done something worse than you, which takes off some of the heat. Even better is having several older teenage siblings; nothing the younger siblings did could match their transgressions.

With so many teenagers, the opportunity for tension seemed to be in a multiplicity of everyday events. The young teenage girls started with wanting to get their ears pierced, which brought on a dissertation about how "your body is a temple of the Lord." The parents eventually acquiesced, but it was not a given.

There was concern about the length of dresses and skirts, and the height of tops (tank tops were out of the question for either sex). Many bathing suits were returned, even though the girls argued they were not returnable. When that was the case, they still could not wear them, since the bathing suit did not have "an appropriate fit."

During the teen years, boys had long hair. Our mother sent us back to the barber if she felt the cut was not short enough. The obligatory warnings were also enforced, "Stay away from tobacco, alcohol, drugs, and sex, and please turn down that noise." Phone rules were easy, "You have been on the phone much too long, you have to get off. What if a patient or a physician consult is waiting for your father?" That worked for sure.

Then there were the teenage runaways who came to our house for a few days. One situation was when a high school friend of the twin girls hid under one of the boys' beds on the third floor, since the girls' rooms and our parents' bedroom were on the second floor. The runaway moved between the teenage boys' room and the storage room. When she was finally discovered, it was very quiet for a week on those two floors.

On another occasion, a high school boy ran away and made residence at our house. By this time we had practice, so the anxiety level seemed lower until the police showed up at the front door. The police officer told our mother he had good reason to believe that the runaway was living in our home. Of course my mother's gut reaction was "Well, that just can't be so." None of us will ever forget the sound of the police officers walking up three flights of stairs to investigate. Naturally, the runaway was hiding under a bed and was easily found. The runaway calmly thanked our mother for the hospitality, and said he would probably see her over the weekend. However, we did not see him at our house for a long time.

Nothing beats teenage squabbles than fighting over who gets to drive the car. We inherited our grandfather's car after he passed away, since we were not allowed to drive our parents' cars. It was a 1970s white Ford sedan with a red interior and the loudest idle ever emitted by a car. Yet it always ran. It served as our car when we took our driver's license test. In fact, many teens in the neighborhood passed their driver's license in this car. It was the good luck car for every new driver test. How could a state trooper fail someone who had a mini St. Michael statue on the console and The Green Immaculate Mary Scapular hanging from the rear view mirror?

Our parents had few boundaries for the car; they were content that we were not bugging them to use their cars. So, the car went everywhere: trips to the Jersey shore, the Pocono Mountains, college campus visits, concerts, Big 5 college basketball games, and high school parties. Given there were four or more eligible drivers at any given time, the car ran from 5:30 a.m. until midnight (later on the weekends).

One weekend, after playing an all-night card game in our basement, we ran out of money early and decided to spend the winnings at the local 24-hour burger joint. To avoid starting the car in the driveway and waking our parents, we pushed it down the driveway and a half a block away before turning on the engine. When we arrived at the fast-food restaurant, we discovered that the gas tank was empty. This was common as nobody wanted to put more gas in the car than what they would use. Some days we swore the car ran on fumes. That night we made it to the hamburger shop but did not have enough gas to get home, even though it was less than a mile. We had to stay with the car all night until the gas station opened at 6:00 a.m. It was a cold night to sleep in what we called "The Funky Ford."

Picking up a girlfriend for a night out was problematic when sharing the car with that many siblings, because chances were someone else was on a date or wanted to cruise with friends. Our parents wisely did not involve themselves in these negotiations. They only weighed in on one need—school—which took precedence over any other need. Teenage dating was awkward enough, but how do you explain to your date that you have to take another couple along or drop off a few friends of your sibling first before going to the movies? In a funny way, the situation worked out to everyone's benefit. It was not an anomaly to have dated the same girl as one of your brothers or to have one of your friends date two of your sisters—at different times of course. The change up was efficient, as the outsider already knew our parents as well as most of the family. With so many big families living in one neighborhood the odds were good that you would have true mixers. One family in particular had five of their six children match up with at least two who were crossovers.

## "WHEN YOU WAKE UP, GET UP. WHEN YOU GET UP, DO SOMETHING!"

"When you wake up, get up. When you get up, do something." This pithy advice was posted to the right of the kitchen door that led outside to the back of the house serving as a reminder to not leave the house until all of your chores were done. Surprisingly, our parents did not have to cajole or "bug us" to do chores. We figured that was the least we could do for these two joyful, loving, and giving souls. The problem arose over the timing. My mother was the master of timing, and her clock ruled. We, on the other hand, tried to do the chores taking our good ole' time, when we were good and ready, causing a clash of objectives.

When it snowed we knew we would have to shovel the driveway, but we wanted to make some money first. As a result, we left immediately after the last snowflake had fallen, and shoveled the neighbors' property for some serious cash. That lasted only a few times, since our father confiscated our earnings. We learned to labor at home first before trying out our entrepreneurial skills.

After her first cup of coffee in the morning, our mother would ask, "Let's see what needs to be done today." As if she did not know. She needed no reminders and knew every task, when it needed to be done, and who was assigned to it.

If something needed to be done off schedule, she was quite political about the situation. For example, the kitchen windows may be a few weeks away from the scheduled cleaning, but she would say, "It is getting harder to see out that window. Does that window look clear to you?" Or, "My, my, the dust sure does build up fast in this part of the room." Or, "I was thinking about giving this porch a nice sweeping." The other memory skill was when we said we would do something "later." She had a natural time clock for when later came; she did not forget the promise.

## "EVERY CHILD, NO MATTER HOW MANY, IS SPECIAL."

Our father was commissioned into the U.S. Army Medical Corps in April 1946 for almost two years of active duty, eventually gained the rank of captain. He was fortunate not to have seen active combat, as he worked as a chief of laboratories at the Army Hepatitis Research Center, 120th Station Hospital in Bayreuth, Germany.

Our family had someone in four of the five military services. Our oldest brother joined the U.S. Coast Guard. His military experiences proved invaluable especially during the summers when he taught us how to navigate all kinds of boats, read nautical maps, and identify what the flags meant on various vessels and marine patrol stations.

Another brother joined the U.S. Navy and was on a major aircraft carrier, where he was a helicopter crew member going on rescue missions, which included jumping into the vast ocean waters.

The fourth child and third son joined the U.S. Marines at age 17 in the 1960s, thus was deployed to Vietnam immediately after boot camp.

In the late evenings during those years, if you went to our parents' room, the lights would be off, but there was a faint light from a burning cigarette. Our father would sit in his favorite reading chair in this room with rosaries in hand. When asked what he was praying for he said, "For your brother to come home safely." Thank God he did.

For as our mother always reminded us, "Every child, no matter how many, is special."

# ACKNOWLEDGEMENTS

Our family populated the full range of the baby boom era (1945-1964). Much has been written about the baby boom era given the remarkable number of children born during this period. Not all parents of this era had big families, but many did. Many references are made about large-size families in literature, movies,

*"Some people seek happiness; others create it."*

TV, sometimes in the news, and sometimes in jest or disparaging ways. However, little has been captured about the heart and soul of large-size families and "how they are run," in any time period, even by the sociologists and demographers. This book is an authentic look at big families and how we lived, from a multiplicity of everyday events.

Like many things we learned in life from our parents, this book is a collaborative effort. While putting it together was the major task of our brother, Stephen, we all celebrate and enjoy sharing the wonderful memories and experiences of our family, and our amazing parents who made them happen. Their legacy still lives in our hearts and with our families.

We knew many large families; they are too numerous to mention. We salute these parents for their dedication, wisdom, self-sacrifice, creative child rearing, good humor and most of all good graces.

As you got to know our stories, we would like to acknowledge who we are: Joseph (1945); Mary Beth (1946); Gregory (1948); Mark (1949); Concetta (1950); Frances Ann (1951); Elisa (1951); Denis (1952); Mario (1954); Angela (1955); Margaret Mary (1956); Stephen (1957); Marita (1959); Susanne (1960); John (1962); and Ann Marie (1964).

Thank you to our editor, Trish Shea, for not only helping to maintain the craft of good nonfiction writing, but for capturing the true spirit of this book.

Made in the USA
Middletown, DE
10 March 2016